A History of the Ideologies of the Welfare State

With special reference to Canada

Dave McFaul

A History of the Ideologies of the Welfare State
with Special Reference to Canada

Amazon - Kindle Direct Publishing

ISBN: 9781796247121

iv

Preface

The first chapter explains that when a university modernized to become a research institute, modeled after Germany and Austria, the philosophy department turned to idealism. Idealism then inspired the secularization of the social sciences into History, Political Science, and Economics as separate disciplines. While the intellectuals did not come up with the idea of the welfare state, they were used by the government to man the welfare state. After the fact, and for the longest time, there was a consensus between socialism, liberalism and conservatism on the need for the welfare state. I go into the past arguments in depth as a task of retrieving a way of thinking that no longer seems to be with us.

The second chapter of the book deals with what has been the dominant ideology 'til today, neoliberalism. Hayek showed that the communist economy collapsed because there were too many details for a central committee to coordinate and command. He also created the Mont Pelerin Society of international think tanks to be ready with policy advice for when the Keynesian hegemony faltered. Friedman toppled it off its pedestal. It was accepted there was a trade-off between unemployment and inflation. When both increased during the 1970s stagflation, Friedman argued we were stalled at the natural rate of unemployment anyway so we should instead concentrate on increasing the money supply at 3 to 5% annually for a policy named monetarism. According to Friedman, Keynes was also wrong about the Great Depression. It was not the result of a glut in demand but of drastically shortening the money supply. It was the result of government interference, not the free market. In the 1980s neoliberalism produced a paradigm shift such that the welfare state was cut back, though it could not be completely eliminated. It was too popular.

The third chapter relates that the rationale behind the welfare state went through a sea change for the left. Risk had shifted from being government and corporate responsibilities to becoming the concern of private individuals. Healthy risk taking became a mark of heroism and as Foucault said we were to be entrepreneurs of ourselves. The state was to encourage this by investing in such 'human capital' as health and education, while legislating to promote free markets where they weren't before. However, Mandelbrot has shown that markets are a lot riskier than theory says they are, and there remains a need for pooling collectively to insure ourselves against risks that can financially ruin us.

1: The Birth of the Welfare State

Studying history is like looking at a fractal. One can see off-hand a general pattern, but one can also zoom in to examine a vast amount of minute detail. What is interesting about history is its contingency and complexity; important decisions are often affected by the personalities and relationships of the people involved. W. H. Dray (1993) argues that history is not a positivist science. He followed Collingwood in arguing that when historians discuss causation they are not referring to sufficient conditions that produce an effect in a law-like manner, because nothing is guaranteed. Historically there may have been compelling reasons making an action rational, but the agents involved had to interpret their situation and decide how to respond. When historians talk about causes they mean that without the cause the effect would not have happened. There can be other roads to the same destination. "A narrative identifies episodes, phases, stages, steps, advances, setbacks, anticipations, turning points, watersheds." (Dray, 1993, p. 105).

The historical thesis of this chapter is that the modernization of the university, after the German model, led to the welfare state in Canada. Every time a university modernizes to become a research institution rather than a clerical one, its philosophy department goes through a period of idealism (Collins, 1998). This philosophy inspired the ideologies that formed a consensus after the industrial revolution, when they became Democratic Socialism, Social Liberalism, and Red Tories, and all agreed on the need for the welfare state. I look at the most important books for illustrating and defining these ideologies for Canada from the early turn of the Twentieth Century. The story begins with fairly general considerations of philosophy and ideology, but as the main event draws near the contributing concrete historical details become more

2

intricate. As intellectuals gain power, they used this power to gain more power. The texts that I look at performed work in shaping the political tradition from which I come with questions for them to answer. Gadamer calls this historically effected consciousness. The task is simplified by studying Canada a small country where more remote and extreme ideologies have less traction.

*

One of the purposes for developing higher education in Canada was to continue British culture and traditions in the new colony. In the 1840s, the colleges were at first denominational schools enabling students to debate against heresies. The Anglicans had Huron College and Bishop Strachan. The Methodists had Victoria College and Egerton Ryerson. The Baptists had Acadia College and the Presbyterians had Queen's and Knox. The Ontario government funded the University of Toronto so that it was 'officially' secular and allowed to award degrees, taking law and medicine away from apprenticeships. It was also intended to inculcate Christian values. Eventually the denominational colleges ran into financial difficulties and amalgamated with the University of Toronto (U of T) for provincial funding. The atmosphere at these places were what Foucault called 'complete and austere institutions,' totally regimented like monk's cells. Evangelism was everywhere. Being born again had varying degrees and styles according to the denomination. Student life involved atoning for one's sinful desires through the 'self-improvement' of subordinating selfish interests to duty. Intellectual development was subordinate to the moral education of the future professional. Respect for panoptic authority followed by strict obedience was to enable the personal conversion of the students who, at the time, came mainly from the farms.

The focus was primarily introspective, which was reflected in the philosophy of 'Scottish Common Sense' that organized the curriculum. The writings of Thomas Reid and Dugald Stewart tried to refute the skepticism of Hume by appealing to our direct observation of common everyday experience. We are confronted with the object itself, not separated by Lockean 'ideas,' and this can be discovered through a direct appeal to our consciousness. We can turn to the 'empirical' data of our consciousness to explore the different physiological faculties of the mind, such as the active intellect of moral intuition and the passive intellect of inductive knowledge. The study of science is justified by Paley's natural theology, as revealing God's providence in creating the laws of nature for the benefit of life. There were no specialists, lab equipment was nil with maybe a microscope if the university was lucky, and there were few experiments. There was no call for rationalism, materialism, or new research projects. The Ancient Classics were central to the curriculum as indoctrinating the student with the basic foundations and

A History of the Ideologies of the Welfare State

values of the Western tradition, including politics, rhetoric, drama, philosophy, history, and geography. Studies that were not directly practical, such as learning dead languages, were justified as exercising the intellectual faculties of reasoning and communication. By the 1860s, English literature had been introduced to develop skill at combining the faculties through exercising the imagination, while also facilitating historical knowledge of the English/Scottish tradition. Scottish Common Sense philosophy justified a general and broad education for gentlemen scholars.

What shattered this age of orthodoxy was Darwin's **On the Origin of Species** published in 1859. It replaced Bacon's inductive method of drawing tables of similarities and differences to create a taxonomy. It enabled discovering the contributing factor which varied in proportion to the presence or absence of what was being studied, to explain the variance. For Canadian professors

6

this was to reveal the plans and laws of God. Darwin went beyond Bacon's humble inductive method by offering speculations and the method of hypothetico-deduction; deducing consequences from a hypothesis for empirical testing such as the data uncovered from digging up fossils. Darwin suggested that evolution from a prototype, or genotype, can account for the variety of species according to random mutations and the resulting survival or extinction of that variation. Divine providence was not needed to account for evolution and the tables of variance for biology were contingent. It opened up a number of debates in newspapers and periodicals between the claims of science and religion. Those who had faith in arrogant reason, according to the Christian Guardian, a Canadian Methodist journal, would not see the need for Divine mercy and revelation (McKillop, 1979, p. 122). Technological progress gave strength to science's claims for independence. Many were conflicted about the proper relationship between Christian faith and empirical proof. Once the issue was raised, however, people had to answer the question.

In the 1870s and 1880s, W. D. LaSeur used Comte and Spenser to offer a dualist answer, compatible with Scottish Common Sense, which argued for the freedom of science as an independent critical reflection to dispel superstition, as long as it acted responsibly in service to the incommensurably higher moral realm of the organic community, within which individuals functioned and had their purpose. The problem was experiments on the brain made the separation of mind and body problematic, weakening traditional Christian ontology. Common sense was no longer the final court of appeal but needed testing and critical evaluation.

Idealism and the Modernization of the University

The philosophy that provided the desired answer was the Hegelian Idealism that accompanied the transition of the medieval university into a research institution modeled after the 'German university.' Randall Collins (1998) explains that at the turn of the 19th Century the Prussian state was a centralized bureaucracy that had mandated elementary schooling, and further demanded formal credentials for hiring staff, creating a hierarchy among the older disciplines. The *Gymnasium* was absconded to train students for the state-sponsored university and those who wanted to teach at these secondary institutions had to have a university degree. The medieval university was a suitable vehicle because it had developed its own topics and methods of argument, while sponsoring creativity through the competition of public debates in the attempt to attract more students, and through the practice of dissertations along with their defense. The state-university enabled a highly productive level of technical specialization that would not have been appreciated or sponsored by a lay public. It used to be that philosophy was merely a preliminary for theology and law. The increasing status and sophistication of philosophy within the university, along with the growing number of its teachers, supplied the ammunition needed to fight for academic autonomy freed from the constraints of orthodoxy and doctrine. The new official power of the university, in training an upwardly mobile professional class, made taking it over a strategic move, securing future careers for other philosophers. "When other German universities emulated the Prussian model after 1810, there were no more university failures, and enrollments rose fairly steadily." (Collins, 1998, p. 650) The German universities continued a path of controlled expansion until 1900.

Wherever universities become modernized and make the transition to becoming a research facility, the move is accompanied by the development of Idealism in their philosophy departments: England, Scotland, Canada, America, Italy, Scandinavia, Japan, and even France (Collins, 1998) (Gutting, 2001).

Germany had three major Idealists:

- **Kant wrote *The Critique of Pure Reason (1781)*** to fight off rational metaphysics and Pietist occultism. The former, inspired by Leibniz, is deterministic and causation is to be a pre-established harmony. The latter claims supernatural revelations in the mediation of God. Kant wanted to ground claims to knowledge on sensory experience while refuting Hume's skepticism. We can only know the world as it is for us, not the world as it is in itself, speculations that go beyond this lead to antinomies, contradictions and paradoxes. Mathematics is *a priori* but it is not just analytic, relying on the non-contradiction of stipulated definitions, since formulas give scientists a true and accurate representation of real relations within the empirical world. Math is a true synthetic *a priori*, a necessary presupposition for the intelligibility of any possible experience. Philosophy can explain the epistemological pre-conditions needed for any science to be considered valid, allowing empirical research projects to multiply unimpeded and reveal concrete details.

- **Fichte wrote *The Science of Knowledge* (1794)** giving birth to Idealism as a popular philosophy in the German university by linking it to spiritual considerations. He proposed investigating the necessary ontological presuppositions assumed by the ability to identify and contrast different things. Opposites are synthesized by revealing the ground that allows for oppositions, such as the self that postulated an opposition. The opposition can then be contrasted with the Self, which is defined as pure abstract consciousness. Thus, the Self freely posits itself in a circle, and knowledge entails reflective self-awareness. To further propose, as some do, that the knower and the known are together in the Absolute has religious implications. It resembles Johannes Tauler's Trinitarian description of the ground of the soul in deep meditation, where the Father posits the Son/Word who returns to the Father as the Holy Spirit in complete surrender and blissful satisfaction. The idea came from Fourteenth Century Germany and greatly influenced the Pietists.

- **Hegel wrote the *Elements of the Philosophy of Right* (1821),** and opened the social sciences to philosophy through a historical narrative where the limited oppositions of earlier ages are qualified and put in perspective by a later, more comprehensive understanding. History is the progress of reason and freedom. In it Hegel applies his dialectic to law, politics, and economics. The important message is that individuals are who they are by being situated in a living community and tradition. Punishing violations of property law are overcome as morality induces people to act responsibly. What this means depends on the relationship either family or business. For Hegel, both styles of relationships are needed for legitimate government, and are to be incorporated within the brotherhood of a corporatist government offering the different ways of life, or guilds, their own representation for negotiating the conditions under which they lived.

In the transition from the Prussian and German example to the Canadian uptake, there was British Idealism. The importance of this form of Idealism was not so much about defining the place of knowledge and argument within the modern university but in creating an ethics and a political philosophy which eventually formed the basis for the welfare state.

English Idealism had four important ethical and political tracts.

- **F. H. Bradley's first book *Ethical Studies* (1876)** promoted communitarianism and saw the end of all action as self-realization.

  The problem with hedonism is it conceived pleasure apart from that which gives pleasure. By focusing on mere subjective and transitory feelings, we concentrate on haphazard and disconnected instants. We lose sight of the self as a whole, a persistent overall cohesive pattern. Hedonism is excessively particular.

On the other hand Kant wanted duty for duty's sake, but we can't carry out a notion of duty that is purely abstract. We have to will something particular and any act can be shown to accord with abstract rules. Laws can conflict, so in a particular circumstance any rule could be broken. There could not be any duty apart from our particular duties.

Bradley went between the horns of the dilemma by postulating a 'concrete universal' in our station and its duties. We are born inheriting characteristics from our family and race. Our whole life we are being constantly educated so what we think and feel is a social product. Language shapes

16

our thoughts and characters, and carries the sentiments of our society. In adulthood, our identity is determined by our station and social role. We become who we are by our relationships. Apart from the wider whole we are mere abstractions and incomplete. Our social self is our true self, and we can only truly realize ourselves through society. This is universal but only exists through the details of our actual duties. As a concrete universal it is a whole which incorporates diversity.

We rise above our lesser self by living up to our station, but we may not achieve self-satisfaction because of the state of our society. As rational beings we have to stand back and reflect upon this to improve it. Thus, the ethics of self-actualization has a political side, though it is true that science and art help reflection and should be pursued for their own sakes without having to refer to political interests. We are not pawns and can have lives of our own, it is just that we are ultimately constructed by our relationships, which is where we find our fulfillment and self-realization for the most part.

- **T. H. Green's *Prolegomena to Ethics (1878-1882)*** preached the 'common good' and was published posthumously in 1883, edited by Bradley. Green, as well as Bradley, begins with the ideal of self-actualization. Our freedom consists of contrasting our actual self with a potential self we attempt to make real. Instead of asking 'what should I do?' we should ask 'what should I be?' This will call for the complete realization of our capacities, our perfection.

18

However, as we grow so do our ideals. We may not be able to tell the ultimate aim from which we fall short, but if we look at history as the evolution of the divine spirit within us manifested in our institutions, we can see progress and some things were really better than others. Moral ideals explain the facts of moral effort as bringing about the kingdom of God.

Our pleasures depend on the happiness of others, so we can't become better persons without sharing ourselves with them; not as a means to accomplish our pleasure, but as ends in themselves. The common good does away with the dichotomy between egoism and altruism. It doesn't involve competition, where some win at the expense of others. It is a spiritual good because material goods involve scarce resources which necessitate conflict. Therefore, the good is

something to be or do, not something to have.
With a common good there are no losers. It is best
thought of as a single project which combines
dissimilar roles like a symphony.

Contributing to the common good is adding
to something larger than us, which may last
beyond our deaths. In ourselves, we are only
potentially people; it is only in a social context that
we become complete. We help shape society,
which in turn helps us be who we are. Spiritual
progress only means something when it is manifest
in the lives of individuals. It therefore cannot
command their extinction for something greater.

- **Green's _Lectures on the Principles of
Political Obligation (1879-1880)_** was
published posthumously in 1885-8. It is less radical
than the Ethics; he does not recommend coercive

taxation to pay for charitable projects, because the potential for human perfection needs the freedom to act voluntarily.

Green's interest in the 'rights' of the citizen and of the state earned him a place in the tradition of English liberalism. The citizen has a right to life and liberty and property, while the state has claims that supersede the individual for purposes of war, punishment, and moral improvement. The real value of our institutions is to enable our moral capacities to be realized.

A moral life depends on the will to freely determine our satisfactions for ourselves, rather than being driven by external forces, and on the intellectual understanding of the common good, where each helps the other achieve their excellence. Society has a claim on individuals to do their duty, which in the end is perfecting their character, but to do this individuals have to claim the right or freedom to do their duty. It is only through the freedom of rights that individuals can accept the common good as their own and act to achieve it, which in turn is what justifies their rights. This means recognizing the rights of others, as well as their recognition of our rights, as something shared.

Rights are made by recognition. A right is a power claimed and recognized as contributing to the common good. It is only as the organ of the general interest that the popular vote can endow any law with the right to be obeyed. Resistance is to be done only for the public good, not because the majority want it. It is in submitting to the law that one learns not to be a slave to momentary desires and imposes on oneself what one should want.

Citizens should not remain passive recipients of protection, however, but should be involved in maintaining the state. Their patriotic motive should be a passion based on a common-dwelling place with its associations of common memories, traditions and customs as well as common ways of thinking and feeling that a common language and culture embody. Rights may not be tangible, but the power of states are subordinate to them. Not just any coercive power can be sovereign. Only power exercised in a certain way for certain ends makes a state, according to the rule of law for the maintenance of rights.

The 'General Will' of society depends on the hopes and fears of a people bound by sympathy, a sense of possessing common interests and of acting together for common ends. The more complete the range of possible actions and the more people who can enjoy such freedom, the more complete the political society.

- **Bernard Bosanquet wrote *The Philosophical Theory of the State* (1890).** According to Bosanquet, our true self is not what we are but what we should be. We are more than what we have become. We imperfectly try to be what we ought to be, our real self; as against laziness, ignorance, and stubbornness. The constraint of our everyday will is an oppression, the limitation of our possibilities. We are not supposed to be able to do whatever we want, but be what we really want to be. We are enslaved when we yield to temptation but are free whenever we conquer it. We can be distracted by goals that will not satisfy us, instead of focusing on an object which represents the Self as a whole, free from contradiction and at our maximum. Our center of gravity is to be thrown outside ourselves into a self we want to be, rather than what we are. 'We can will what we want but not want what we will.'

Criticism involves adjusting partial goods to harmonize them with the whole. We go wrong through narrowness and confusion, abstracting out of the whole. Instead of fleeting pleasures, in society we gain new concerns beyond the self that offer a purpose and stimulus to life. The State can be defined as the operative critique of all institutions. It is the only recognized and justified use of force. We rely upon the state to support, extend, and correct our conscious will. We are extended by the knowledge, resources, and energy of society beyond what we are aware. The state can use force to arbitrate claims and adjust the claims of individuals and their social groups which is best done without any physical violence.

Through reasoning and persuasion, it is possible to regulate claims and ensure livable conditions in society. The State can also be seen as the 'hindrance of hindrances,' as taking away obstacles to self-conscious development. Anytime there is a better life struggling for self-actualization, the deadlift of interference can remove an obstacle that holds people back. "Why not … hinder unemployment by universal employment, over-crowding by universal house-building, and immorality by punishing immoral and rewarding moral actions?" (Bosanquet, 1890, p. 177) According to Hegel, the meeting point of individual minds is the 'social mind.'

> An institution implies a purpose or sentiment of more minds than one, and a

> more or less permanent embodiment of it.
> 'Of more minds than one.' because it is to
> fix the meeting point of minds that the
> external embodiment is necessary.
> (Bosanquet, 1890, p. 277)

Our institutions exist as 'ethical ideas' capable of

critiquing us as we are, and arbitrating our claims

through discussion, persuasion, and recognition.

Later, Hobhouse (1918), while accepting

Green, argued against Bosanquet that by

combining the idea that we are only free when we

control ourselves with Hegel's idea that the

Objective Spirit is the society created by a people's

own self-made history, we would be completely

abdicating our freedom, self-will and conscience to

society as it is rather than as it should be.

The transformation of Idealism into Political Economy during the industrial revolution in Ontario

Hegelian Idealism dominated Canadian philosophy from the 1870s to the First World War. The University of Toronto hired George Paxton Young in 1872 as a known Scottish Common Sense philosopher from Knox, where he taught 'Logic, Mental and Moral Philosophy' and 'Evidences of Natural and Revealed Religion' for eleven years, but he converted into an influential teacher of Berkleyan Idealism. The most important philosopher was John Watson at Queen's University. He arrived in Canada in 1872, having studied under the most prominent of Scottish Hegelians, the preacher John Caird and his younger brother Edward. (Edward Caird wrote an introduction to the fifth edition of Green's *Ethics*.) Idealism rejects dualism and gives science a role within the rational development of moral society as a part of the history of

28

spiritual progress. Instead of individual atonement, it popularized a notion of self-actualization where the individual realizes their full potential in furthering the goods of society. This inspired the mission work of the social gospel, which sought to establish a New Jerusalem on earth, eventually leading to the United Church of Canada and the CCF/NDP. It did not rely on scripture, or tradition, and downplayed denominational concerns and born-again evangelism. In proposing a rational religion, it opened the way for secular research to eventually take over the social sciences.

At the same time, between 1870 and 1890, Ontario underwent an industrial revolution. Science and technology were seen as essential to economic progress, but these academic subjects had been developed as a Christian defense against Darwinism. The older generation had been British gentlemen scholars, and the demand for new technical research was combined with a nationalist

A History of the Ideologies of the Welfare State

call for hiring young Canadian graduates. In 1877 James Loudon delivered his presidential address to the Canadian Institute commending the U of T to adopt the German research ideal that had proven so successful at Johns Hopkins University in the United States. There needed to be an increase in professional staff, student assistants, and facilities to help researchers specialize more productively, and this depended on a secure and stable increase of financial contributions to the University by the provincial government. There was also a general demand among academics for PhD programs, as a way of generating more research and assistants. The School of Practical Science was formed in 1873 – by 1884 it could award the degree of Civil Engineering. It officially became part of the U of T in 1889. The Kingston School of Mining and Agriculture was established at Queen's in 1893. The Ancient Classics became marginalized by the expansion of English literature as the means of transmitting cultural values.

30

At the U of T, mathematics and physics were separated in 1887, and the next year 'English and History' became 'English' and 'Political Economy and Constitutional History' chaired by W. J. Ashley, which also weaned it from under Paxton Young's chair in 'Mental and Moral Philosophy.' Ashley was a safe choice, dedicated only to objective academic research. He left for Harvard in 1892, leaving the post to James Mavor. In 1894, 'History,' headed by Reverend George Wong, became a separate discipline distinct from 'Political Economy.' In 1888, John Watson had secured Adam Shortt an appointment to teach Political Science at Queen's. Shortt held the Sir John A. Macdonald chair of Political Science from 1892 to 1908, when he became the first chairman of the Civil Service Commission until 1917. According to Carl Berger (1956), apart from Wong, Shortt was the one responsible for the early development of Canadian History. In 1908, O. D. Skelton replaced his mentor Adam Shortt at Queen's and

A History of the Ideologies of the Welfare State

Stephen Leacock became Head of Political Science at McGill. In the beginning Ashley, Mavor, Wong, Shortt, Skelton, and Leacock were the elite, defining the first generation of Canadian social scientists at the turn of the Century.

Doug Owram (1986) explained that in the debate on prohibition at the turn of the century, the justification for non-interference was not based on a first order principle of freedom, as in the USA, but was problematic because prohibition used coercion rather than education and could undermine the independence needed to develop a moral will of self-improvement. Adam Shortt worried about business fulfilling its social obligations, but criticized socialism for promoting selfish class interests. Both would place the individual's material welfare above the social good, and side with the partial over the whole. Shortt's ideal for protecting the public interest was for trusts and unions to be run by impartial boards of experts,

32

an educated elite armed with facts, not theoretical convictions. He did not see his empirical research as being at odds with his mentor John Watson's Idealism, but was instead focused on accumulating detailed information. For men like Shortt, environmental conditions were still secondary to moral improvement. This made him 'old school,' closer to the Idealists.

Political Economy and the Ideological Consensus

Because of the industrial revolution, political ideologies tended to be concerned with economics, particularly class interests and conflicts. The emphasis on the material environment and the value of efficiency distinguished Political Economy from Idealist Philosophy. Canadian political parties have a consensus on the need for a welfare state. It is just that the different ideologies have distinct reasons for supporting the same policies,

A History of the Ideologies of the Welfare State

which can have practical consequences with different nuances.

There have generally been three main political ideologies in Canada which correspond to the names of the different parties, though they are not the same thing and the parties have not conformed to strict dogmas. According to standard textbooks, conservatives favor gradual change, liberals promote freedom and a limited state, while socialists cater to intervention and amelioration through collective ownership. All three came after the industrial revolution.

The welfare state was already in place before the three ideologies were used to justify it. They were justifying policies that were imposed for other 'political reasons' anyway. Intellectuals did not come up with the idea of the welfare state. The German conservative Bismarck created the first welfare state to undermine support for unions, after having outlawed the right of

34

assembly. Canada was late in developing its programs compared to England or Germany (Kuhnle, Frank and Kaufmann, Franz-Xaver, 2010, pp. 72-74).

Germany had Sickness and Maternity benefits in 1883; Accident Insurance in 1884; Old age, Invalidity, and Survivors' pensions in 1889. This was before Eduard Bernstein wrote *The Preconditions of Socialism* in 1899; he was well within the German idealist/communist tradition from Hegel and Marx.

The United Kingdom brought in Accident Insurance in 1897; non-contributory old age pensions in 1908; Sickness or Maternity benefits in 1911; and Unemployment Insurance in 1911. The last two came into being when Hobhouse's *Liberalism* went into print (1911); he was both inspired by Green (1879-1880) and critical of Bosanquet (1890).

A History of the Ideologies of the Welfare State

Only Accident Insurance existed in Canada before Stephen
Leacock's *Unsolved Riddle of Social Justice* in 1920;
the government instituted it first in B.C. in 1902.
Other programs followed in time: non-contributory
old age pensions in 1927; Alberta medical care in
1935; Unemployment Insurance in 1940; and
Family Allowance in 1944. The last three policies
were contemporary with the heyday of Democratic
Socialism's or Social Liberalism's intellectual peak:
Keynes' *General Theory of Employment, Interest
and Money* was printed in 1936, then the Beverage
Report for social insurance in the UK came out in
1942, followed by the Marsh Report for Canada in
1943.

• German Democratic Socialism –
Eduard Bernstein (1899)

The definitive statement of Social Democracy is Eduard Bernstein's *The Preconditions of Socialism* (1899/1993) also translated as *Evolutionary Socialism*. It is 'revisionary Marxism.' According to Marxist science, there is a class war and revolution is historically necessary. However, economics is not the only effective cause in history, and Bernstein did not think the proletariat, or blue-collar working class, would be the chief driver of change. They live in crowded conditions, are badly educated, unorganized, with uncertain and insufficient income. Violent revolution is not inevitable, and democracy is not to be compromised for a dictatorship of the proletariat. Increasing democratic control is an end in itself and the form in which socialism is to be realized, not merely a means to overthrow the system. Grass roots self-government is the precondition for emancipation. The

Social Democratic Party is to be concerned with the common good, not only the interests of industrial workers, and the rights of all minorities must also be protected. There is room for private enterprise in a socialist economy, and there is to be no expropriation without compensation. Bernstein also thought 'market socialism' should support consumer cooperatives which benefitted the whole community.

Marxist theory has it that wealth will concentrate into fewer and fewer hands, while the masses become poorer and poorer. Bernstein saw there was both an absolute and relative increase in the number of property owners. Big business did not swallow up small ones, and there was no reduction of the middle class. Industry was increasing in specialization with an increase in the division of labour, so governments are better able to regulate businesses than run them all. The precondition for socialism in the centralization of industry was only partially achieved. The other missing precondition for socialism was that workers were not a homogenous mass, but highly differentiated with tenuous feelings of solidarity. Different occupations entail different life styles. Only a few can have aspirations beyond improving the conditions of their own work, and not all workers care for communal ownership. Trade unions can enable workers to have more say in the workplace while protecting them from wrongful dismissal, but they should not form a monopoly against the community.

According to Bernstein, there is no conflict between socialism and liberalism. By expanding people's economic rights, socialism is advancing the universal expansion of the franchise. Minimum wages and limiting the number of working hours may curtail freedom, but only to increase total liberty. According to Bernstein, socialism cannot deny the Manchester idea that those who can work are responsible for taking care of themselves. No freedom without responsibility. However, social services in the form of public schools, unemployment insurance and mutual aid societies can help soften the harshness of self-reliance. We do not have a 'right to work,' but no one should be forced to sell their labour under conditions that are not acceptable. Collective bargaining and arbitration must be compulsory. Parliamentary reform through elections and piece-meal legislation is secure and safe. Engels thought the socialist party should do what it can for the poor, but not undermine the need for revolution. For Bernstein proceeding cautiously and pragmatically will avoid violent experimentation, regression and failure. This inspiration for slow and peaceful progress came from the Fabian Society the think tank for the British Independent Labour Party (ILP).

• **English Social Liberalism – Hobson (1909) and Hobhouse (1911)**

In 1909, J. A. Hobson wrote *The Crisis of Liberalism: New Issues of Democracy*. He wanted to supplement the haphazard and piecemeal approach of political opportunism with a broader vision and philosophy of liberalism. Among his observations were: small remedies produce no tangible results. Detractors against the growth of government services, or those lukewarm and undecided, are afraid of the socialist rhetoric that condemns rent, interest and profit. They are afraid private enterprise and individual freedom will be overcome by state bureaucracy without any real benefits. According to Hobson not all industry can be taken over by government. Family businesses might grow to become monopolies that will have to be taken over by the state to protect consumers from unreasonable prices. Other industries cater to tastes that are so unique to the individual that they cannot be made routine enough to be run collectively and have to remain an art. Alfred Marshal explained that some businesses grew big because of economies of scale, others remained small because of diminishing returns. If a monopoly is the result of economic conditions, then they cannot be broken up without having them return to a natural monopoly. If it is the result of a tariff or licence, then these can be rescinded. The only alternative to a natural monopoly is public ownership.

The main reason for the government to offer a service is to increase the people's equality of opportunity. This entails a positive support for freedom involving more funding and state activity than the merely negative liberty of non-interference. Everyone should have a right to a piece of land they can work or live on, without the liability of being turned out at the will of another. This means being regulated by a public authority, not the whim of a landlord. A lack of mobility can hinder someone from obtaining work they want. The nationalization of railroads and highways enable those in less populated areas to be charged as little as those living in more populous areas. Utilities like electricity and water are natural monopolies which have to be nationalized to keep prices from being discriminatory extortion. Credit must be available to those who face an emergency, so they will not fall prey to the loan shark, and the ordinary man who needs to invest in their business should be able to do so with governmental loans.

The ordinary person is not free because they are not secure, and need insurance. A person can find themselves out of work through no fault of their own but because of disease, a downturn of the economy, or a shift in technology, etc. Few of these can be foreseen. Government is in the natural position to offer wide-scale insurance backed by the public coffer. Justice demands equality before the law, but this is compromised when those with more wealth can win trials because of it. There has to be recourse to counsel provided by the state. Self-development depends on equal access to knowledge and culture through free libraries and cheap literature. Poverty or the need to earn a living should not keep a child from school, or someone from pursuing higher education. Education should not be a narrow ladder but a broad easy stair. Universities should not be forced in doctrinaire directions because they are funded by the clergy or business. Education produces greater industrial efficiency and enables other benefits to be established and become fruitful. We need to train great leaders and discerning citizens. This is more important to society than simply training for a higher paying job.

*

In 1911, Leonard Trelawny Hobhouse drafted a book simply called *Liberalism*. He placed himself within the tradition from Bentham to Cobden, Gladstone and John

44

Stuart Mill. After discussing the history of liberalism he ended on T. H. Green, whose view he described as organic or harmonic. While it is true that liberalism holds the majority should not suppress the individual, it is also true that we should help each other to achieve more liberty than we can on our own. The former is negative liberty; the latter is positive liberty. Following Green, while Hobhouse thought there was nothing in society above and beyond, or behind, individuals interacting with each other, he thought that if we separated individuals from society, important parts of them would cease to exist. For any claim to be right it must be sound in the eyes of an impartial observer, who must take account of the good for everyone, and insofar as his judgement is rational it will have to be based on principle. Therefore, rights cannot conflict with the common good, nor exist apart from it. This does not assume a harmony which already exists and only needs prudence for its effective operation.

The organic view sees harmony as an ideal as well as a reality. We try to move toward harmony as the natural impulse of feeling and action, even if the goal goes beyond our present reach. The common good involves each individual developing their personality to the fullest: "the widening of ideas, the awakening of the imagination, the play of affection and passion, the strengthening and extension of rational control." (Hobhouse, 1911, p. 71) It is this that makes life worth living and makes society a living whole. It postulates and constitutes a common will. Everyone should "enter into the common life and contribute to the formation of a common decision by a genuine interest in public transactions." (Hobhouse, 1911, p. 117) It further upholds that "the formation of such a will, that is, in effect, the extension of intelligent interest in all manner of public things, is in itself good and more than that, it is a condition qualifying other good things." (Hobhouse, 1911, p. 118) People may appreciate something because it is the result of public deliberation. The full fruit of social progress is achieved when citizens are not passive recipients but active contributors. Thus, the goal is to make rights and responsibilities real and living, as well as to extend them as widely as possible. The ideal society is the harmonious growth of its parts, each developing on its own according to its own nature and in the process furthering the development of others.

In the absence of legal restraint, the strong can coerce the weak in a free contract. Therefore, liberty is not secured by the absence of law but by its promulgation. When all has been said and done to secure the individual's freedom of conscience, the conscience of the community must have its way. The state must listen to the individual's conscience while the individual must respect and live within the state, abiding by its laws. Hobhouse outlines many of the services of the welfare state, such as "educating the children, providing medical inspection, authorizing the feeding of the necessitous ... helping them to obtain employment ... the mitigation of unemployment, and providing old age pensions." (Hobhouse, 1911, p. 83) The state is not so much to clothe, feed and house the poor, but to provide the economic conditions where they can do this for themselves. A worker is not responsible for the ups and downs of his industry, but is its victim just the same. Therefore, it is justice, not charity, to help. It used to be thought that self-help would be adequate but this faith was undermined by history. There has been a significant improvement in the living standards of many, but workers are still not able to provide for all the possible emergencies which can ruin them. The system of industrial competition has failed to provide a living wage that can support a healthy and independent existence that is the birthright of all citizens of a free state. However, the conditions of the overall economy can be influenced by the organized action of the community. To this extent Hobhouse's liberalism was socialistic.

But liberalism does not assume all value is the result of labour, or that there is a class war with a clear-cut division between rich and poor. It also does not agree that the masses need to be led by an *avant garde* elite. The liberal is not to govern others but work alongside them. The state must not suppress personal growth but ensure the conditions for the self-maintenance of a normal healthy individual, guaranteeing them a job by which they can support themselves and their families, as well as a minimal social safety net. The state must provide the means to avoid destitution. The independence of the citizen will not be undermined, since the sustenance provided by the state will not be enough to meet all their needs. They will still have to work. But this will still offer some hope, security and a brighter outlook. There will always be those who will abuse any situation, but people are more effective when the burden on their shoulders is manageable. Charity will make one dependent on the good will of another, but when support is a matter of justice this won't have the same effect. When people can't earn enough to support themselves, it is a matter of justice.

The rich *should* be taxed to support the poor. People must be remunerated enough for them to continue their industry, but beyond that is a surplus that belongs to the community. The community provides infrastructure, skilled labour, accumulated knowledge, technology, inventions, and, not least, demand for their goods. Society is an indispensable part of the creation of wealth. The individual does not do it all on their own, as much as they would like to brag they did. One may make better use of resources than another and should be compensated accordingly, but to ignore the input of society will deprive the community of their just share in the fruits of industry, resulting in a one-sided and inequitable distribution of wealth.

It has been said that speculation on stocks does not contribute anything productive to society; such profit could be taxed without stopping the practice. Inheritance can similarly be taxed, as well as a 'super-tax' on extreme incomes. In this way tax is not taken from an individual who has an unlimited right to call their income their own, but is a repayment due to society. Public expenditure must benefit all classes, but some are not fit for work including the physically incapable and mentally defective. The objective should be to make them independent and self-supporting, and giving them a chance would enable them to contribute to society. Improving the conditions of the working-class will also benefit society as a whole and in the end pay for itself. The ability of the state to supervise the general economy must be set side by side with economic justice. Progress is more certain when pursued

A History of the Ideologies of the Welfare State

piecemeal rather than by the destructive methods of revolution. Decades later, T. H. Marshal (1950) argued that history was marked by a progression from legal rights like *habeas corpus* to political rights like the Magna Carta, then finally to economic rights, such as the welfare state.

- ## The Canadian Red Tory – Stephen Leacock (1920)

Red Tories seem to be a Canadian phenomenon when compared to the United States. But the German conservative Bismarck created the first welfare state with compulsory insurance for sickness in 1883, accidents in 1884, with disability and pensions in 1889, to undermine support for unions, after having outlawed the right of assembly. Gad Horowitz (1966) noticed that socialism is a live option in Canada, but dead in the US. What little there is in America is doctrinaire Marxism, not a Canadian style which is modeled after the British Fabian Society. He

52

attributed the difference to the conservative-tory tradition in Canada, as opposed to the United States who took the liberalism of Locke as an absolute foundation against anything 'un-American.' (Canada has more tolerance for ideological diversity.) The split began with the United Empire Loyalists. Both socialists and Tories see society as a corporate-organic whole that is more than an agglomeration of competing individuals pursuing happiness in a purely self-regarding way. Canada did not have a lawless, individualistic-egalitarian frontier. They deferred to authority, believed in monarchy, and desired 'peace, order and good government'. The Canadian conservative tradition believes in the common good and noblesse oblige. Since the creation of the railway to unite the country after Confederation, Canadians have been more willing to use the government to develop the economy. Because of the French population, Canada has sought to protect group rights as well as individual ones.

A History of the Ideologies of the Welfare State

Stephen Leacock was a true conservative. He believed in imperialism, though he wanted Canada to be more than just a colony; and held such regressive attitudes as to want to deny women the vote and keep ethnic minorities from immigrating to Canada. In 1920 he wrote *The Unsolved Riddle of Social Justice*. He argued against both the old-fashioned liberal individualism of classical economics and the new-fangled utopia of socialism. Leacock complained that with all of the labour-saving devices we have created we are still overworked and underpaid. With the technological increase in our productive power, people are still starving. We under-produce necessities to create more luxuries than we need. There is a discrepancy between the potential of our economic power and the satisfaction of our needs.

In classical economics, given the enforcement of contracts and private property, by following our self-interests society would be better off under *laissez-faire*.

54

Equilibrium is where supply equalled demand. If the price is too high, competition will lower it; if too low, producers will seek other opportunities. Strikes can do nothing to affect minimum wage. Under free competition and individual liberty, everyone earns what they are worth and are worth what they get. Classical economics thinks everything sells at cost. The cost of production is determined by wages while wages are limited by the 'natural' price. This is a circle that explains nothing. According to Leacock it is not true that everyone gets what they produce. Instead, payments are the result of competing forces of 'economic strength,' Leacock was a student of Thorstein Veblen's at the University of Chicago, who in turn was influenced by the German Historical School. If a monopolist charges an exorbitant price few can afford it, but if he lowers the price until it is common, profits are eliminated. A monopolist will limit the amount of his goods to a point that can maximize his profits, which will not be enough to satisfy everyone's needs. An employer will only pay what they have to, which will depend on the scarcity and organization of labour. The more workers are unemployed and the less organized the less the boss will have to pay for them. Overall, the consumer will insist on paying the least price. The producer will charge as much as possible while also paying the lowest wages. And, the labourer will ask for the highest wages. The result is an unstable equilibrium that will be upset for any number of reasons. Whatever social advance has been made by the masses is the result of the organization of labour. So much for economic liberalism!

Leacock turned to socialism. He saw the call for the collective ownership of the means of production as a naïve panacea that would lead to disaster if put into practice. He felt outlawing socialism would be counterproductive, it would be more effective to bring its fallacies to the light of day through open discussion. The only real problem with socialism was that it could not work because it expected more altruism than men were capable of. He stated that in criticizing society, the socialist loses sight that society actually does work. Private ownership has been demonized into being the source of all problems. Democracy is fit to run the government, but not everything else. Under socialism, work will have to be directed by elected bosses, and directors are wrongly assumed to be impartial toward themselves and their friends. This is too ideal. Although the average person can be hindered by accident of birth and a lack of education, they are still their own boss. Under socialism either everyone's wages are the same, or there is inequality. With inequality, the glib persuasive talker can gain all the good positions for themselves and their friends without merit, through elections and appointments. With equality, there is little incentive to work harder or save for a rainy day, the state will take care of everything for everyone.

A History of the Ideologies of the Welfare State

Socialism assumes wrongly that everyone will want to work, but the worker will have to work where and when they are told or be punished.

It is also true that the idea of 'everyone for themselves' no longer held. The First World War showed conscription is the duty of every citizen, but along with this came certain obligations from the state. Unemployment is a social crime. If no work can be found for every able-bodied person, then it has to be provided. There must be pensions for the old and insurance against illness, accidents, and infirmity. The war taught a sense of solidarity. A nation which neglects this cannot survive against one where the welfare of each contributes to the safety of all. Even the purest selfishness will dictate a policy of social insurance. The risk of economic loss must be shifted from the individual to society at large. The effort put into dealing with the rare exceptions of famine, flood or pestilence must be used for everyday matters.

58

There has been talk of conserving natural resources, but the most valuable resource to conserve is men and women.

The strength of a nation lies in its citizens, so it is important to protect those who are born. Malthus would have us believe that any attempt to help the poor will only lead to over-population. Every child has the right to be housed, clothed, fed and educated irrespective of their parent's lot. "The ancient grudging selfishness that would not feed other people's children should be cast out." (Leacock, 1920, p. 129) These children will fight for the billionaire bachelor or spinster so the obligation should go both ways. Every child should have equal opportunity and should not be crushed by lack of food or premature labour. It may be too late to help the adults, but not the children.

Just as war justified progressive taxation so it should during peace for the betterment of the population.

A History of the Ideologies of the Welfare State

It will come back two-fold. This is not socialism because it doesn't cover everything. The vast bulk of industry will still lie outside the immediate control of the government. Each person will have to earn their own living. 'Natural economic laws' are unjust and intrusive legislation should adjust conditions so each decade is an improvement upon the last through regulating minimum wages and hours of work.

*

In Canada there are two main ruling parties, the Liberals who tend to attract progressive votes and the Conservatives who attract more right-wing voters. Other parties, such as the New Democratic Party, which serves social democrats, also exist. All practice brokerage politics. They downplay social cleavages in order to portray themselves as the national party of accommodation, not democratic division. The single member plurality system ensures the major parties have more seats than their percentage of the vote, but ridings are still regionally based. In order to appeal to a small population scattered over a large territory, they have to be catch-all parties that avoid extremist policies which will alienate people. This means the parties are not doctrinaire but shift positions, including adopting policies which they have previously opposed. Liberals campaign to the Left but govern to the Right, while Conservatives sometimes find themselves to the Liberals' Left as Red Tories. Intellectuals may feel partisan polemics undermine their academic freedom and credibility. They aim for consensus. Except for Question Period, ideological conflict is muted and complex. Committees depend on conciliation and compromise.

Social Security for Canada 1900-1945

The assumption that contributions to social improvement should be voluntary was put into question by industrial growth and the accompanying increase of population within the cities at the turn of the century. Manufacturing equipment had made farming less labour-intensive while plants needed workers to man the machines and service the auxiliary businesses. Between 1901 and 1911, 125,000 to 200,000 individuals left the rural areas (Owram, 1986, p. 18). It had always been assumed the future of Canada was in agriculture and people worried about the collapse of rural life, wondering what happened to the individuals exposed to the city. Sanitation and housing became major concerns as people started to notice the slums. The individual who had some autonomy for self-sustenance on the farm would find themselves prey to a multitude of interacting variables: low pay, poor housing, bad diet, and disease. The social gospel offered a new moral mission and crusade in fighting for a collective intervention to alleviate the suffering. Unfortunately, it soon became obvious that the need was too great for the Churches to successfully organize.

Reformers needed government programs. Shortt's successor, O. D. Skelton, wrote *Socialism: A Critical Analysis* (1911), arguing that government action could relieve some of the problems and conflicts that led to radical socialism. If only government would respond.

From 1896 to 1911, Wilfred Laurier was Prime Minister. The elder generation that was leading the Liberal party had been involved with the establishment of responsible government and Confederation. The constitutional battles involved were justified according to the British constitutional tradition of protecting individual rights. Laurier and his senior cabinet ministers did not favor appeals for government intervention. Yet, from 1900 to 1910 the basic principles of collective bargaining were put into Canadian law, largely due to William Lyon Mackenzie King. At the age of twenty-six, he became Deputy Minister of Labour. He began with the Conciliation Act of 1900, but moved toward compulsory arbitration with the Railway Labour Disputes Act in 1903. He was more willing to use legislation than Laurier liked. The defeat of the Liberal government in the 1911 election was the result of Laurier's contemplating the American offer for reciprocity and free trade. Clifford Sifton, once a close friend of Laurier's, sided instead with Canadian manufacturers and used emotions of anti-Americanism and British loyalty to sway the electorate against Laurier. The intellectuals were dismayed because when Canada was finally given a real choice about its future, it had been derailed by corrupt politicians manipulating the populace through propaganda, instead of having the decision based on informed debate with definite goals. The populace needed to be more educated.

At the time it was recognized that Canadian universities needed to offer courses more relevant to commercial needs or they'd lose promising students to the USA, but there was a concern that this could undermine the primary function of the university to transmit critical reasoning skills and social morality. The social sciences needed to be publicly recognized as policy experts with a technical knowledge of efficiency separate from philosophy. In 1912, a university president, Woodrow Wilson, was elected President of the United States, initiating a close alliance between the University of Wisconsin and the government. Before Adam Shortt entered public office he had grown to be one of Mackenzie King's most active labour conciliators. When he entered public life he was one of two commissioners charged with administering the new 1908 Civil Service Act, which was to rationally classify the civil service and promote merit as the criterion of hiring and promotion. Shortt had always complained about the prevalent practice of patronage, but the Act only covered internal headquarters and positions, not the outside majority where patronage was at its strongest. He designed competitive applications, searched for ways to streamline services, and used professors like John Watson to grade the new examinations. The task that lay ahead in trying to organize the civil service was overwhelming, and he got little support from Laurier and Borden, who saw Shortt's role not as an expert but as a standard bearer of integrity. In 1913, the Canadian Political Science Association (CPSA) was formed to create a professional forum for political economists to communicate their findings and come up with policy alternatives. It died when World War I broke out, and in 1917 Shortt resigned from the Civil Service Commission, after a clash with the politicians. Prime Minister Robert Borden moved him to the Department of Historical Publications, where he spent the rest of his career as an historian cataloging the National Archives.

Reform in Canada was just starting to formally organize itself by the beginning of the war. The Social Service Congress in 1914 and the Civic Reform League in

1915 were still dominated by middle-class philanthropists, but in 1915 Newton Rowell appointed the Ontario Commission of Unemployment. The business cycle seemed to be beyond the common sense of the politicians and businessmen. Many political economists from the various universities in the province were sought for input. The conclusion was that the unemployed were victims of an economic depression beyond their control. The province was called upon to provide public work programs and unemployment insurance. It set a precedent for academic involvement, with a corresponding desire to look at environmental factors and the possible need for government intervention and provision. However, this was still to remain voluntary. Just when reform had started to organize, the First World War dissolved these initiatives.

In the beginning intellectuals had seen the war as an opportunity for deep changes. Partisan interests had to be sublimated to a common war effort, which needed expertise to efficiently employ its resources. Democracy had to show its ability to run just as effectively as the German totalitarian state, providing a better society for the veterans who returned. But, as the mass slaughter continued, by 1917 the idealistic sacrifice of the 'nation's best' seemed unending, futile, and self-defeating. The Wartime Elections Act had just disenfranchised any possible dissent from new immigrants, and the Union government was formed to legislate conscription against Quebec's wishes. It seemed to some that the state was willing to ensure victory at the cost of democracy. McKillop (1994, p. 235) writes "as a war of movement in continental Europe [the Great War] lasted only a few months, as one of deadlock and attrition it lasted four more years." The top bureaucrats, bickering among themselves, seemed incompetent to end the war with its horrible waste of human lives. The world seemed to have gone insane, and a naïve optimistic faith in social unity and the progress of reason died. Idealism was over and done.

On the other hand, the war had proven the effectiveness of the university for developing munitions and anti-toxins. In the 1920s, Canada witnessed a growing white-collar middle-class. Programs in commerce were now offered within the Political Economy departments at Queen's and the U of T. There was a steady increase of students for these programs and the Political Economy department was able to expand and hire more teachers. Even more important for the influence of the university on government was the maturing of 'social services.' From the start, Canadian sociology was connected to the University Settlement Project of 1910, modeled after Toynbee Hall in London's slum-ridden East End. It followed the English tradition and was somewhat hostile to the sociology practiced at Chicago. Robert MacIver had been active in the program since 1915 and eventually took over as active director of the department at the U of T in 1918. In 1922 he replaced Mavor as Head of the Political Science department. For MacIver, sociology was supposed to be holistic, incorporating the other social sciences, but as department head he had to manage a number of specialists pursuing very different interests. He revised the undergraduate curriculum into streams that would eventually concentrate on 'Economics' and 'Political Science.' In 1926 he wrote *The Modern State*, which criticized Idealism for turning the state into a metaphysical entity and an end in itself, while still criticising the horrors of laissez-faire. He went between the horns of the dilemma by arguing the State should only intervene for the benefit of citizens through social programs. MacIver left for the USA in 1927 and was replaced with E. J. Urwick, a sub-warden of Toynbee Hall from 1897 to 1903 and the first Director of the London School of Sociology from 1902 to 1910. Under Urwick, 1927-1937, 'Political Economy' became the largest department at the U of T. His attitude was that sociology as an empirical science studied only causation, but social philosophy went beyond behaviourism to discuss the ethical significance of its research for how we should live. Nevertheless, he still remained strictly non-partisan.

In the 1920s, the 'civil service' began to mature. The journals *Social Welfare* and the *Canadian Forum* were created in 1918 and 1920 respectively to facilitate communication among professionals and aid the formation of a professional identity. Graduate training became necessary for employment, and the methodology of case studies was introduced for detached research. The religious orientation was fading and patronage was being replaced by secular merit, but wide-scale reorganization and classification were still needed for equity and efficiency. In 1925, William Lyon Mackenzie King hired O. D. Skelton to be under-secretary for the Department of

External Affairs. He proved to be more successful in effecting change than Shortt had been. As the responsibilities of national autonomy increased, he was able to include more intellectuals in government operations, paving the way for others; delegates had to be sent to the League of Nations and the International Labour Organization. The Dominion Bureau of Statistics was still the center for Political Economists, not the Department of Finance. The advice of social scientists was seen as more valuable for policy implementation than policy formation.

This changed in the 30s when the Great Depression made the social scientists more valuable. Private businessmen seemed either unable or unwilling to help. Canadian historians have paid particular attention to the League for Social Reconstruction (LSR) as a think-tank for the socialist CCF party and the emergence of a mandarin civil service class. The LSR was most famous for the anthology *Social Planning for Canada* (1935) which argued for collective ownership and centralization of the federation. The League also made a case for public medical and unemployment insurance.

More significant, according to Owram (1986), was a new informal network of intellectuals interested in public issues. This new reform elite tended to have at least one degree, in an era where few still finished Grade Twelve, which meant they often came from educated middle-class families. Their activities were generally centered at the university, which gave them a significant bond even when they strongly disagreed, because sometimes they had to come to the others' aid to defend their academic liberty and freedom of speech against politicians and the public, who saw the university as an expensive luxury during the depression (see Francis, 1986, pp. 109-127 for the case of Frank Underhill.) They had studied at Harvard, Chicago, and particularly Oxford for which there were more scholarships available. This gave them a more cosmopolitan outlook than the average Canadian, with international connections to some powerful people concerned with the same issues. They tended to be the new young Political Economists, around age 35, who had been trained in the new social sciences where they learned the scientific method of problem solving; and they found distasteful the emotional righteousness of dilettantes. Though their mission of secular social service had its roots in the religious imperative, material and environmental factors were more important than moral and metaphysical ones. They shared a common experience of disillusionment with the war, many of them having served overseas. Unfortunately, francophones and women were not of this clique.

This 'government generation' was small enough to know each other. There were 25,000 to 30,000 university and college teachers employed during the Thirties; of these less than 150 were social scientists, and even fewer actively involved in public affairs (Owram, 1986, p. 143). Social scientists would use the Canadian Historical Association and the *Canadian Journal of Economics and Political Science* (CJEPS), both formed in 1935, to keep in touch with each other and discuss academic topics. But the CPSA, created again in 1929, and the Canadian Forum had included businessmen and a lot of civil servants, thus extending the academic network by discussing topics that were considered pressing and relevant by the broader public. The Depression made this imperative. There were a lot of clubs and associations during this time, and academics spoke at most of them; understanding the importance of public opinion for a democracy, yet realizing there was a lack of good information. Social scientists started shaping public opinion, increasing their connections and public status in the process.

When it came to academic involvement in politics, there seemed to be a dilemma between the disengaged objectivity of science and the social engagement of politics. Harold Innis worried that the scientist would sell out, offering pat solutions and quick answers that went beyond the limits of established knowledge. He felt critical thinking demanded an autonomy that was undermined by the bias of partisanship. On the other side of the spectrum was Frank Underhill. Inspired by the American progressive historians of the 1870s, Frederick Jackson Turner, Charles A. Bears, James Harvey Robinson, and Vernon Parrington, Underhill pursued an historical search for a Canadian liberal progressive tradition, i.e. the radical newspaper columnist Goldwin Smith. His interpretation involved investigating protests in Canadian history to reveal how the masses have paid for the desires of the few for more wealth and power. He helped create the LSR, originally designed as a think-tank for progressive intellectuals. Underhill was so inspired by the mission and integrity of J. S. Woodsworth, a former social gospeller, that he helped the organization draft the CCF's Regina Manifesto in July 1933, the Magna Carta of Canadian democratic socialism. The CCF was the party of farm and labour. Thus, the LSR became too narrow for intellectuals to use effectively since it was limited to a particular radical party. What were important were the needed programs, whichever party would implement them. Most intellectuals had the choice of either working directly inside the parties, or leading information sessions and 'summer schools' as external professional educators.

Doug Owram (1986) gave two examples of how intellectuals shifted between the parties. The first example was Brooke Claxton. As an intellectual, Claxton renewed his conservatism because he saw R. B. Bennett was at least willing to face the problem of the Depression by using a tariff, unlike Mackenzie King who was too ambiguous and cautious. Bennett was Prime Minister from 1930 to 1935 and had started a Conservative summer school, a multidisciplinary conference for politicians. He had intellectuals in high positions, like Queen's Clifford Clark for deputy minister, who introduced the Finance department to economic planning, and R. K. Finlayson as private secretary, who advocated Roosevelt's New Deal as a model for Bennett's New Deal. However, Bennett was uncomfortable with intellectuals unless their role was well defined, and when questioned he would respond by blustering. Nor did the front benches develop any close ties with intellectuals. Claxton did not think Bennett's New Deal was very well worked out in detail, and the Judicial Committee of the Privy Council (JCPC) declared it ultra vires. Eventually, he collaborated with Frank Scott in writing reform proposals, but did not join Scott in forming the LSR, because socialism was not the answer to a bureaucratic problem – an educated and efficient staff was. He drifted to the Liberal party because he felt King was not as dictatorial and would win the 1935 election. He wanted to see to it that King would not continue his history of deficit reduction. He wanted to recreate the link between politicians and intellectuals that already existed at the municipal and provincial level (in social work, housing, child welfare, health and sanitation, etc.) at the federal level to deal with the Depression, a macro-phenomenon.

The second example Owram (1986) gave of an intellectual shifting between parties was Vincent Massey. When Bennett used a grapevine to fire Massey as Minister to Washington it ruffled a few feathers, as did Bennett`s authoritarian imperialism. Massey was made party president for the National Liberal Federation to create an effective network for that party instead. He went beyond organizing fundraising to cajole King into accepting more active measures. Vincent`s wife, Alice, was impressively well educated on reform issues and would help entertain important political guests. She would, also, often intervene to help restore peace between King and her husband. Inspired by Britain`s Liberal leader Robert Hudson, Massey joined with Norman Rogers and William Dafoe in writing King`s speeches and in creating the Sanhedrin Club to informally discuss the issues of the day, which linked the journalists of the Free Press with the intellectuals and King. Massey also followed Bennett`s example by introducing summer schools, exposing the party`s platform to the public. King did not like this and was upset that Massey had compared the new direction of the party to that of the CCF.

According to Owram (1986), the first step in economic planning was a 'central bank.' Traditional economic theory had it that the economy would always self-adjust to equilibrium, where supply equaled demand in full production and employment. The quantity theory of money held that expansion of the money supply would only affect prices through inflation. Investment would increase the demand for money and interest rates would rise until demand eased off and would eventually drop making investment more attractive. The Depression had been brought on because the war had diverted too much of the currency, making less of it available for other important transactions, and the collapse of the Gold Standard made international exchange unstable. The decline of prices, in 1929-33, hurt farmers with fixed overhead and diminished income. The bankers feared a central bank would become a political tool, introducing inflation and undermining the value of investments. The Finance Act had required no reserves and was under the partisan Department of Finance. Economists felt credit was too important to be left to the commercial banks; a central bank would stabilize price, interest rates, and foreign exchange.

Minister of Labour Norman Rogers introduced banking expert C. A. Curtis to Mackenzie King, and more importantly to Clifford Clark, Bennett's Deputy Minister of Finance, who was already interested in the idea. Clark made A. W. F. Plumtre, as someone involved with Curtis' and Massey's study groups, secretary of the Royal Commission on Banking, or the Macmillan Commission. Plumtre favored a central bank and incorporated testimony from seventeen economists, replacing the bankers as the traditional experts. Bennett established the Bank of Canada in 1934, and Alex Skelton, son of O. D. Skelton, was head of its research department. The bank did not follow policies of easy money because Graham Towers, the assistant manager, felt that inflation would result from debasing the currency and hurt those with fixed incomes.

In the 1920s, King had tried to distance the Federal government from relief programs. These had been unevenly developed by the provinces, which were now facing potential bankruptcy. Alberta had gone into partial

82

default by 1936. Bennett had authorized loans to the provinces, which seemed to have become a bottomless pit for programs over which the Feds had no control. Poor provinces were not able to provide as well as rich ones, but migrants would not qualify due to residency requirements. Ad hoc grants and the `dole` were insufficient. Norman Rogers called for The National Employment Commission (NEC) to register the unemployed and aid provinces with conditional, but secure and stable, grants. While the Commission included some prominent businessmen, Rogers had been moving the Commission toward the need for a National Unemployment Insurance Act when Mary Sutherland objected to King. Afraid of the sensitivity of Dominion-Provincial relations, King told Rogers the report had to be watered down. Finance Minister Clifford Clark argued interest rates had been too high, due to uncertainty, for the provinces to pay back and suggested guaranteed loans by the Feds if the Bank of Canada could oversee provincial budgets, a job too complicated for politicians. Alex Skelton, head of research for the Bank of Canada, thus called for a National Finance Council, or Loan Council, to oversee Federal-Provincial relations. The provinces resisted such centralization.

Abruptly, World War II began in September of 1939, another unforeseen contingent event that changed everything. Entering the war, intellectuals feared that calls for reform would seem disloyal and the aftermath of the war would be followed by the dominance of reactionaries, as had been the case with the First World War. The war also offered opportunities insofar as the Federal government was forced to take on more responsibilities entailing a dramatic increase in civil servants, many of whom were university scholars. The Economic Advisory Committee was established in 1939 to facilitate financial planning, followed by a Committee on Demobilization and

Rehabilitation. In the early years these were too pre-occupied with the details of winning the war to issue reform proposals. Some intellectuals began to raise the issue about a potential lack of accountability of bureaucrats to the electorate, especially when the moral ethos of the social gospel was replaced by one of technocratic efficiency. After the war, Frank Underhill shifted from socialism to liberalism in reaction to the suspension of individual rights and freedoms that took place under Russia`s communism. While acknowledging the problem, most intellectuals felt non-intervention was even more dangerous. It was feared that when the war was over and the veterans came home, the large amount of money that had been saved would be used for consumer goods. If the economy did not react fast enough there would be a shortage of goods, with resulting inflation. If the vets could not find ready work, this temporary boom would end in extreme depression.

A History of the Ideologies of the Welfare State

Reconstruction after the war became an important concern in the early 1940s.

In January of 1941, a Dominion-Provincial conference was held to discuss the recommendations of the 'Rowell-Sirois report' from the previous year, which the Royal Commission on Dominion-Provincial Relations had been working on since its inception in 1937. The report had suggested amending the BNA Act to allow centralized planning. Clifford Clark, O. D. Skelton and Alex Skelton pressured King to implement the proposals immediately. However, the Premiers Hepburn from Ontario, Aberhart from Alberta, and Pattullo from BC made sure it would not go through. Later, when Rogers was shifted from Finance to National Defence in 1939, the displaced minister, Ian Mackenzie, was moved to Pensions and National Health where he was influential in campaigning the ministers to recognize the need for social security, like medical insurance. He also chaired the

Committee on Demobilization and Rehabilitation where he consigned Cyril James, president of McGill, in 1940 to lead a sub-committee, the Advisory Committee on Reconstruction. The result was an interim report for planning reconstruction, which was criticized by the Economic Advisory Committee (EAC) but it had made people aware of the need. In 1942, the renamed Progressive Conservatives held a summer school at Port Hope, which became the party platform for social programs to compete with the CCF and Liberals. In March the same year, the Marsh report was presented by Leonard Marsh to the Commons Committee on Reconstruction, 300 pages presenting Social Security for Canada: children`s allowances, medical insurance, old age pensions, unemployment insurance, etc. Inspired by Sir William Beveridge`s report for the United Kingdom, it was the most comprehensive and successful proposal of its kind, becoming an extremely popular topic among the press and populace. While King was visiting Washington in December, Roosevelt praised the Beveridge Report and suggested that such was the natural mission for the two leaders of North America. Despite his caution as Prime Minister, King had fancied himself a reformer since his early days as Minister of Labour.

The 'tools of reform' were explained by Keynesian macroeconomics. Keynes successfully combined the Nineteenth Century role of the state to facilitate industrial development with the social gospel demand for social improvement. Universal social programs could boost consumer demand without marginalizing private enterprise. King had put in place Unemployment Insurance in 1940, when it was realized that it could be afforded during the wartime full employment and would not be called upon until after the war a few years later. The provinces agreed. In a 1943 election the Ontario Liberals had been replaced by the Conservatives with the CCF as opposition, and the federal Liberals had lost four by-elections to two CCFs, a Progressive, and a Communist. Feeling the pressure, King made Family Allowance central to the campaign of winning the 1945 election. It was an answer from the civil service for infusing cash without upsetting wage and price controls. To show his commitment to the new role of government, King promptly created the Department of Veteran's Affairs and renamed the Department of Pensions and National Health as the Department of Health and Welfare. W. A. Macintosh was made head of a new Department of Reconstruction and issued a white paper explaining the new commitment. According to Owram (1986, p. 317), the intellectual reformers had finally triumphed.

From Idealism to Political Economy to Social Security, the grandchildren of Canadian Idealism inherited a Federal government that developed universal flat-rate Family Allowances (1944), contributory Unemployment

Insurance (1940), universal flat- pensions or Old Age Security (OAS) and a needs-based one with costs shared with the provinces (1952), single payer universal hospital insurance (1957), Unemployment Assistance Act for those not eligible for UI (1956) cost shared between provinces and Federal government, and support for the blind (1951) or the disabled (1954) (Jenson, 2010). In 1966 they became the Canada Assistance Plan (CAP), the Canadian Pension Plan (CPP), and the Medical Care Act (Medicare). These were all shared-cost programs.

Summary

Scottish Common Sense and Idealism not only offered a set of beliefs and methods of argument, they organized the university and gave it its justification. Scottish Common Sense assured us a smug self-satisfaction against heresies, as plain as observing our own consciousness. Idealism entered Canada as a Christian defense against Darwinism, finding a place for science within the more comprehensive perspective of a larger social context. As a colony, Canada has always had a communitarian streak and Hegel fit well. Idealism inspired the social gospel as a rational religion devoted to good works, replacing the evangelistic concern with dogma and being born again. Idealism was undermined as a philosophy, however, by the disillusionment of the First World War. By then, it had given birth to the discipline of `Political Economy` as *the* Canadian social science which attempted to fill in the more concrete details left open by Philosophy after the industrial revolution.

From the beginning, there was an attempt by academics to improve government and implement rational planning. At first this was accepted at the municipal level with city planning over transportation, sanitation, and housing, as a result of a huge influx of residents, the consequences of industrial growth. Before the First World

War this had expanded to the Provincial level in dealing with business cycles. At the Federal level, Adam Shortt had tried to organize the civil service and replace patronage, but he soon ran into conflict and resigned at the beginning of the war. The war began with optimism but as it dragged on it made people question the progress of reason and the rationality of personal sacrifice to the state as the embodiment of social unity. The demise of Idealism was not simply a matter of an increasing sophistication internal to philosophy, but the external impact of a war on a disillusioned populace that now needed to search for more reliable alternatives, popularizing Russell in England and Heidegger in Europe.

Offering courses in commerce, the Political Economy department grew and professional journals were created. The increase in Political Economy that allowed it to mature in complexity was not the result of an essential element at the core of the field, but of an accidental feature contingently associated with the department. O. D. Skelton opened up External Affairs to intellectuals, whose only avenue previously had been the civil service. Another external accident, the Great Depression, proved particularly advantageous for increasing the influence of Political Economy. There was a loss of faith in the private sector as economic experts.

A new generation of Political Economists used journals, clubs, and associations to communicate to a broader public. They began infiltrating the Federal parties, shaping their platforms, writing the leader's speeches, and educating the politicians. The first step was a central bank then, with the onset of World War II, came Unemployment Insurance. Within the last two years of 1943-4 the number of events that effectively added pressure to the government for reform increased dramatically, building on the longer-term trends. Commissions, committees, and conferences during the war made politicians aware of the need for a post-war macroeconomic planning that incorporated social security. The Beveridge Report inspired the UK and the US. With all this talk and after losing some elections, King felt the pressure to reform. After using the promise of Family Allowance to win the 1945 election, he committed the government to economic planning by academically trained experts. Social scientists tried to distinguish themselves from philosophers and philanthropists by emphasizing efficiency; in the end Keynes united them all.

A right-wing critic could argue that the intellectuals were merely **creating** busy work for themselves, when there was really little that could be done. They created for themselves a position of power, authority, and well-paid contracts, based on nothing more than pure speculation. Robin Neill wrote:

> Applying Keynesian economics to Canadian
> circumstances was problematic. Keynes had

> developed his theory on the assumption of a balanced, homogenous, closed economy in a unitary state. The Canadian economy was open, regionally diversified, relatively dependent on primary product exports, and governed by a federated state. (Neil, 1991, p. 173)

Keynesianism did not really develop into a hegemonic economic theory until the 1950s. Even then its full development was in trade theory, with Harry Johnson's work on international exchange rates in the 1960s. As far as welfare economics went, economics was often a justification for policies to which politicians were already committed anyways, rather than real attempts at 'demand management.'

2: Neoliberalism on Cutting Back the Welfare State

The welfare state is not dead. It has proven too popular to be eliminated. Instead it has been cut back or retrenched. The ideology that has justified this retrenchment has been neoliberalism. Many conservatives don't like the term 'neoliberalism' because they associate it with left-wing socialist liberalism. Nothing could be farther from the truth. Neoliberalism is a call to return to the free trade liberalism of Adam Smith and the self-reliance of Manchester liberalism. Instead, these critics prefer to be called 'economic libertarians,' which is misleading because neoliberals see a larger role for the state in enforcing the rules of the market than the libertarians. Incarceration is something the right-wing thinks the government *can* do (Harcourt, 2011). One percent of the American population is in jail. Fortunately, Canada has not relied on tougher penalties as a strategy for dealing with poverty.

Neoliberalism is the product of Friederich Hayek. He argued the details of an economy was too complex for a central committee to coordinate. He also created an international network of think tanks linked to the Mont Pelerin Society. They offered policy alternatives and waited for the time when the Keynesian hegemony toppled. In 1976, with his Nobel memorial speech, Milton Friedman offered monetary policy as an alternative that subordinated the call to 'full employment' to that of controlling inflation. He had also taught the Depression was not a problem of low demand, but of high interest rates. Both have been very influential in Canadian history from Brian Mulroney and John Crow on. The problem with John Crow was that he raised interest rates to an exceedingly high level to kill inflation when Canada was going into a recession, so that he cut off the oxygen supply to our economy, making matters worse.

George Grant's Lament for a Nation (1965)

George Grant was a red Tory saying goodbye to the Canadian conservative tradition. His book *Lament for a*

A History of the Ideologies of the Welfare State

Nation (1965) was the most articulate philosophical expression of red Toryism. He was afraid Canada was losing its independence and being taken over by American liberalism. Just because this may have been an inescapable historical development did not mean it is for the better. Canada was an underdeveloped frontier and the capital necessary for development had to come from the United States. If the terms for investment were tougher, there would be less invested. That would be the quickest way to undermine the economy of the nation. The crucial years that undermined Canada's sovereign independence were during the early forties. Liberal policy under Howe was to integrate with the US as fast as possible and become a branch-plant economy. The dominant classes saw themselves at one with the continent. It was true that the support of the elite was not enough, the people had to vote the Liberals in, but where were people to learn any alternatives when the newspapers and TV bombarded

98

them with already processed opinions? Foreign capital was capable of determining governments and their policies by incarnating themselves as the indigenous ruling class of Montreal and Toronto. After the war, during reconstruction, governments never questioned the authority of business to run the economy. No government would last long otherwise. Capitalism was based purely on profit-making, even at the expense of virtue. Nationalism that would restrict free trade was seen as counterproductive in closing markets to the powerful. According to Grant, the rich felt they lost nothing of value in losing the independence of their country which had begun during WW2 because Canada needed to be unequivocally united with America for defence against the Axis. This continued during NATO. Canada should fairly support international defence, of which Americans just happened to be the hegemonic leaders.

A History of the Ideologies of the Welfare State

According to Grant there was more to it than Canadian history. He was inspired by the political philosophy of Leo Strauss, particularly the contrast between the Ancients and the Moderns. For the Moderns the pinnacle of political striving is the universal and homogenous state. Universal because a world-wide state will eliminate international war, and homogenous so everyone is equal and there will be no class war. This will be achieved by science, which will conquer human as well as non-human nature. Where science dominates there is no room for local culture. Marx believed in progress where we will eventually eliminate scarcity so humans will no longer exploit each other. This will end alienation and the conflict between personal freedom and social order. Technology will serve the human good. Liberalism will deny any goods that limit the freedom to do what we want when we want. Values are subjective and we choose our own good. In private, every taste should be allowed so long as there was no public inconvenience. But in public there is no pluralism of taste, the conquest of human and non-human nature is the only value. Either one found their role in public engineering or retreated into the privacy of pleasure. This is limited by Marx's ideal of the perfectibility of man since greed will have to be restrained for the common good. Marxist socialism only triumphed in totalitarian regimes that need discipline to industrialize. In the West, the Protestant work-ethic does not encourage any desire other than acquisition, but technology has enabled other passions to flourish along with greed. Except for scientists and executives, the work ethic has disappeared, but the political power of the elites is reconciled with the private satisfactions of the masses. Liberalism enables the stability of constitutional government with a doctrine of God-given human nature. Whereas totalitarianism taught men are completely malleable to perpetual conditioning and invasive control.

A History of the Ideologies of the Welfare State

The West has respected individual rights more than the Eastern tyrannies, but corporations have destroyed indigenous cultures in every part of the globe, just not as fast as Communism.

Grant argued it was no longer possible to be a conservative in this age. The United Empire Loyalists were not 'selfish and unfortunate men who took the wrong side.' Conservatives like Milton Friedman have more to do with the 19th century liberal rights to use property however they wish within a minimal state, than with traditional conservatism which thinks the community has the right to restrain freedom for the common good. "If they are not committed to a dynamic technology, they cannot hope to make any popular appeal. If they are so committed, they cannot hope to be conservatives." (Grant, 1965, p. 65) With science it is impossible to conserve anything for long. All institutions and standards are constantly changing. Conservatives can only defend those

102

structures of power that are necessary for technological change. But Canada was only possible by a determination not to be part of the American republic. They believed society required a high degree of law and order as well as a respect for public virtue. This means the state has wider rights to control the individual than the US. Canada is less lawless and has a greater sense of propriety. They are considered dull and stodgy, anathema for the progressive mind set. Nothing is more alien than the 'emancipation of the passions.' Public order and tradition is more important than freedom and experiment.

> Canadians have been much more willing than Americans to use governmental control over economic life to protect the public good against private freedom. To repeat, Ontario Hydro, the CNR, and the CBC were all established by Conservative governments. (Grant, 1965, p. 70)

The first government to govern Canada was the Conservatives. They injected capital to unite Canada by building the trans-Canada railroad. Canadians ever since

A History of the Ideologies of the Welfare State

have been more willing than the States to use big government to build the country and its economy. In the end, to ask whether continentalism is progress, or the universal and homogenous state is a tyranny, is to beg the question. Lamentation is between utter despair and absolute certainty. Grant left the question open.

Friederich Hayek (1899-1992)

Hayek thought the feelings and appeal for nationalism, protectionism, and socialism are irrational leftovers from primitive tribalism. He thought community is a mirage and all that exists are individuals, and the only thing which unites them are economic transactions. Hayek is the father of neo-liberalism. He argued (1967) that while a democratic government may be totalitarian, a liberal government may be authoritarian. Justice can only meaningfully be applied to human action that is deliberately brought about by somebody. Since nobody distributes income the results of the market are neither just nor unjust. The market does not correspond to merit or need, and social justice is only a demand for protecting vested interests. We should accept the outcome of the markets even when the results are not in our favour, even when we cannot have foreseen the outcome for which we are not responsible. After the collapse of Russian Communism, it seemed common sense that Hayek was right. A command economy can't work, the details are too complex for a committee to predict and control. Anthony Giddens argues the left has to become friendlier to markets. He wrote: "the left has to get comfortable with markets, with the role of business in the creation of wealth, and the fact that private capital is essential for social investment." (Giddens, 2000, p. 34)

Hayek's Politics (1944, 1960)

Hayek's most famous book is *The Road to Serfdom* (1944). He said he was seeing the same progression of ideas in Britain and America that he had seen led to Nazi Germany. Keynes thought men of good will could use dangerous means for the greater good. Hayek warned men of good will had prepared the way for a regime they hated. Fascism was not a reaction against socialism but was the same conditions that led to the totalitarianism of Communist Russia. The developed democracies at the time thought the progression toward socialism was inevitable. But it was not, it was just that everybody wanted it. If they could see the consequences of economic planning they would shrink back in horror. However, it is not enough to point out the dangers. We need to understand the enemy and perhaps change our ideals.

It is not that the Germans were vicious and it is not enough to hate everything German. Thinking so will only blind us to the real threat. The real problem is liberalism has been driven out by centralized planning. In the book, Hayek saw the need for social insurance, so he was part of the ideological consensus, his main object of attack was centralized planning, thereby against Keynes. Planning can't be contained within defined boundaries because everything in the economy is interconnected. There is no middle ground between free markets and totalitarianism, as Keynes seemed to be offering. Hayek also argued Keynesian 'full employment' is inflationary; undermining real wages instead of cutting the weekly wages protected by unions. Driving demand through the multipliers from investments in infrastructure and public works, while lowering interest rates to increase the money supply for easy loans, is inherently inflationary. Keynes thought the trade-off acceptable.

According to 'Principles of a Liberal Social Order,' a lecture Hayek gave at Tokyo's Mont Pelerin Society in 1966

(1967), liberalism is derived from the discovery of a self-generating or spontaneous order in social affairs. A spontaneous order will have more complexity than a deliberate arrangement. The details are too complicated for a central authority to understand and use properly. The government should be limited to enforcing those rules which will enable spontaneous order. They will be abstract and without full concrete detail, and not directed to particular ends. The alternative is turning purposeless spontaneous order into a purpose-oriented organization that ensures what was more important is not sacrificed to the less important. Rules are simply to prevent unjust action, which is the infringement of someone's rights, especially those of property. This entailed only negative liberty and the disallowance of laws that can't be properly universalized, as Kant said. The rule of law is not a command legitimately ordered but one equally applicable to all. It is not the source of power but the limitation of power that prevents arbitrary coercion.

Distributive justice does not treat everyone the same but according to different rules aimed at particular results for particular people, such as progressive taxation. The just price or wage is one that is achieved without fraud, violence or privilege. A just result is the result of just conduct by everyone concerned. A just market is not one of 'perfect' competition, only one without barriers to entry and which adequately spreads information about opportunities. This will bring more of the dispersed knowledge of different members into play. The coercive functions of government are only to enforce the proper functioning of the market, to secure the competition needed to steer it efficiently. According to Austrian economics, markets develop over time, and entrepreneurs create new needs. Therefore, it is important for governments to lay the ground rules for free markets and enforce them.

In *The Constitution of Liberty* Friedrich Hayek (1960) used the Roman contrast between a freeman and a slave. Freedom from domination means not being subject to the arbitrary will of another. One can be a slave and still be lucky enough to avoid interference and restriction. One's master may not feel like interfering, perhaps because the slave has ingratiated themselves with them through abject servility. Even in the absence of such meddling they may still be subject to possible arbitrary domination. However, Hayek argued that since the employer-employee contract, as well as the relationship between a husband and his wife, are voluntary and there are available alternatives, these do not call for state interference. He did not promote socialism or militant feminism. What he was against was legal positivism where the only thing that makes the law right or obligatory is that it is backed by force, and the law is whatever the legislature says it is. One can be free while being restrained by the law. This happens when the law is not arbitrary but serves the interests of those affected. The law can protect someone from the arbitrary interference of someone else. Properly constituted law defines freedom. Rulers are limited by constitutions that give us the balance of powers, sets term limits for the rotation of offices, and defines the responsibilities of representatives.

Following this understanding of liberty from domination, Hayek had some complaints about the Welfare State. He thought that theoretically it is feasible and possibly fair, but in practice it has its problems. Unions should not be able to force a closed shop where no one can cross the picket line. However, this takes the teeth out of unions and denies to them what makes them effective. Hayek thought inflated wages merely kept others from being employed. As for inflation, it is the result of government policy, which steals from the most vulnerable by lowering the value of their fixed incomes. Progressive taxation and redistribution does not treat everyone equally; taking from some against their will to give to others. Social insurance brings the old imperative of providing for the destitute up to modern standards. With the growth of cities, provisions can no longer rely on neighbourly ties. A central institution had to be created that can provide for wider scale needs. Unfortunately, it is a monopoly that would take care of all needs at once at the cost of inefficiency. It is perhaps inevitable that the state will provide for those who should otherwise make provisions for themselves, even enforcing self-provision where possible so the poor do not become a burden. While it was originally sold as insurance, it became the means for redistribution and the equalization of wealth. The apparatus grew to be so complex that only those who approved of its principles would become expert enough on its workings to critique it. We lose sight of the importance of gradual and unintended evolution, current knowledge can be used to prevent new knowledge from emerging. The taxes used to pay for social insurance is also used for propaganda, to manipulate public opinion to pay for even more provisions we may never use.

Hayek gives specific programs their own criticisms: pensions, health care, and unemployment insurance.

1. Pensions have become necessary because inflation has eaten away at savings, mandatory retirement means those who could have provided for themselves are not allowed to do so. Those who work are forced to provide for those who don't, so with an increasingly aged population pensions can become increasingly burdensome, and eventually exceed the government's ability to provide.

2. Health insurance presents unique problems based on needs that have to be balanced against the cost

of providing care. These decisions have to be made by the sick or someone else. Hayek was against a single scheme that provided free health services for all. There is no objective standard to tell how much care is needed in any particular case. With the advance of technology there is no limit to what can be offered. Health has to be balanced against other needs. Health benefits are no longer geared only to increasing productivity in work, but for the alleviation of suffering and prolonging a life that may no longer be productive, thereby increasing the burden on society and taking up hospital beds. Doctors who used to be responsible to their patients are turned into public servants that get their orders from the state.

3. Unemployment can be alleviated by more flexible wages and higher mobility, both of which are undermined by a system that promises a

percentage of what the worker used to get paid. Some unemployment is inevitable and those in a certain line of work should subsidize those out of work in it, otherwise those in the profession may increase beyond what is needed. This is exacerbated by union pressure for higher wages, especially when they shift the responsibility for unemployment onto the state. The unions should be made to provide for the unemployed in their field. The crises of social security are the result of turning the relief of the poor into a minimum standard of living for all. Hayek favored a means test, against the claim that the beneficiaries should not be made to feel inadequate and they get the product of their own effort or merit. Once created it is doubtful social insurance programs will ever be dismantled. They are inflexible.

Hayek ended *The Constitution of Liberty* with a postscript 'Why I am not a Conservative.' The conservative can only hope to slow down change, not alter its direction. The liberal wants to eliminate obstacles to spontaneous evolution. This can demand radical alterations. The conservative fears change, while the liberal welcomes it even if they didn't know where it will lead. The liberal has faith the market will adapt to new conditions. The conservative is more likely to rely on the oversight of strong authority. He is not against coercion or arbitrary power so long as it is used by good men for good purposes. Conservatives lack the 'political' principles that would enable them to work with those whom they disagree while pursuing different ends. Coercion must not be applied even for moral purposes. The conservative is more likely to blame democracy and a lack of deference for our problems than unlimited government. The conservative distrusts theory and lacks the imagination to help them in the war of ideas. While the liberal does not favor the new because it is new, they will not deny ideas because they upset cherished morals. The conservative is a nationalist favoring protectionism, while the liberal believes in international free trade, especially in ideas. The liberal will not hold they have infallible God-given beliefs they should impose on other nations imperialistically. Hayek did not call conservatives the stupid party, but it would follow from what he had said.

Hayek's Views on Knowledge (1945)

In 1945 Hayek wrote 'The Use of Knowledge in Society.' It is an explanation of cybernetics or decentered coordination, chaos turning into self-organization. A lack of information can be helpful when dealing with overwhelming details. Knowing the cost of a price will help planning investment and consumption, without needing to know why it is the way it is. In marginalist economics if we are given a set of preferences and complete knowledge of available means, marginal rates of substitution between any two commodities will be the same for all different uses. This is not given to a single mind who can work it all out. They are dispersed bits of incomplete and frequently contradictory knowledge which all separated individuals possessed and secured the best use of resources known for ends only they know. Who will do the planning? Competition is decentralized. Will we have to gather all knowledge and transmit it to a central authority or give people such knowledge as they will need to coordinate their plans? If a scientific body of experts can command the best knowledge available, who are the experts? Any individual will have an advantage over another because they know unique information that can be used advantageously, like arbitrage, and if it is left up to them they will do so. Knowledge is supposed to be given and at the command of everyone, but irrationally it isn't.

So long as things go as expected, there will be no new economic problems requiring a decision. Usually economic problems only arise at long intervals when a factory is to be erected or a new process introduced. It is too easy to dissipate the differentials for profitability, and with the same technical facilities one can produce a wide variety of costs. It isn't the law of large numbers, with the mutual compensation of random changes. A continuous flow of goods and services need constant deliberate adjustments in light of circumstances not known before, for unexpected needs. This can't be turned into statistics. Abstracting from minor differences and lumping together items which differ, statistics can't take direct account of the specific circumstances of time and place. Decisions have to be made by the 'man on the spot.' The real problem is rapid adaptation to changes in time and place, to be left to those who know directly of the relevant changes and the resources available to meet them.

We cannot solve this by first communicating it to a central board. A central authority cannot make use of the inarticulate know-how of local residents. This would leave the problem of how to communicate such information as needed to fit decisions into the whole pattern of changes in the larger system. All that is significant is how much more or less they are scarce, and how much more valuable are alternative investments. They don't need to know why things are the way they are. The way the price system works, anytime a small adjustment has to be made in the allocation of resources the merchant will not have to go through the calculation again, going over all the relations between ends and means that might be affected. There is no need to know where the more urgent need is, and how to husband the supply. If people are aware of a gap they will fill it, and this will spread throughout the economy. Those bringing about substitutions do not have to know what causes them.

Limited individual horizons sufficiently overlap so through many intermediaries the relevant information is communicated to all. What a single mind might do is dispersed among everyone involved. How little will participants need to know to take the right action? While economizing on the effort to inform oneself of all the relevant causes, they will move in the right direction. Those who call for conscious direction may not believe something has evolved without design to induce people to do the right things without being told what they are. Civilization advances by extending the number of important operations we can perform without thinking about them; we use formulas, symbols and rules whose meaning we don't understand to take advantage of knowledge we do not possess. Nobody has yet succeeded designing an alternative. The individual can choose their own pursuits, and freely use their own knowledge and skills better than under central direction.

A History of the Ideologies of the Welfare State

Adam Smith said the price system could induce the individual to serve the general interest, while seeking their own private interest. The factors of production do not depend only on consumers' goods, but also on the supply of several factors. Only to a mind given all the facts will the answer necessarily follow, but the facts are never so given. Knowledge is dispersed among many people. A solution is produced by people who possessed only partial knowledge. To assume all knowledge is given to a single mind is to assume the problem away. We can't deny the imperfection of man's knowledge, and the need for a process by which knowledge is constantly communicated and acquired. Mathematical economics with its simultaneous equations assumes people's knowledge corresponded to objective facts, which leaves out what is to be explained. What many do is to spell out what the conditions of a rational allocation of resources must look like and say they are the same as the conditions of equilibrium in a competitive market.

John O'Neill (1998, p. 134) asked:

1. Does price communicate all the information relevant for coordinating actions? And

2. Is the communication of price all that is necessary for coordinating action?

The answer to both is no. In a competitive economy the simultaneous distribution of information about supply and demand and the suppression of the mutual exchange of information about planned responses has led to over-production. Both follow price when what they really need to know is future demand schedules. Price does not communicate all relevant information. In a complex changing economy, there is necessary uncertainty about future demand schedules. As well, the knowledge of the entrepreneur is local and aware of changes here and now when opportunity arises. This cannot be universal, abstracted from particulars. Global markets replace knowledge, local and practical, with abstract codified information transferable across distinct cultures and contexts. Where markets meet traditional societies indigenous knowledge is undermined. The market encourages calculability. Quantification is well suited to communicate beyond the limits of locality and community. Knowledge open to quantification reduces choices to ones with a single unit of comparison. However an audit culture can be just as bad as centralized planned economies. Gathering all the traditional inarticulate knowledge from the past and classifying, tabulating, and reducing it to rules, laws and formulas is impossible. Thus, the free market is open to the same objection as a planned economy.

124

The Mont Pelerin Society (1947)

'The Intellectuals and Socialism' (1949/1967) was Hayek's rallying cry for creating the Mont Pelerin Society two years earlier. The intellectual is neither a 'scholar' nor an 'expert.' They need not have any special knowledge of anything in particular nor be particularly intelligent to be the purveyor of ideas. What qualifies them are the many subjects on which they could talk or write. They just happen to have become acquainted with latest ideas sooner than those to whom they address themselves. Because they are listened to with respect on their native subjects, they are listened to on other topics. Intellectuals "decide what views and opinions are to reach us, which facts are important enough to be told to us, and in what form and from what angle they are to be presented." (Hayek F. , 1949/1967, p. 180) It has little to do with the merits of any real achievements. They have no direct responsibility for practical affairs, and the resulting absence of firsthand knowledge sets them apart from other writers and speakers. Nevertheless, it is their views that determine what will matter in the future.

The intellectual is drawn to socialism by intelligence and good will, rather than 'selfish interests and evil intentions.' They take a model that has worked well in one area to use it in another. It is all very abstract and remote from anything practical. The 'climate of opinion' would make one conclusion rather than another acceptable without a real understanding of the issues. The less specific or precise, the wider the influence. Nietzsche said a lie is a useful fiction that can lead to new investigations. Specialists who achieve public fame can be 'cranks, amateurs, or even frauds' in the eyes of their peers, but in the eyes of the public are the best-known experts. Socialism came from the idea we can organize nature, so we can organize society by applying engineering techniques as a single coherent plan. But what may bear fruit in one field can have limits to its usefulness, and be harmful beyond that. If the intellectual gets the better of an argument, valid objections to specific issues will be brushed aside. The intellectual is uninterested in technical details or practical difficulties, but is into broad visions. Yet they can end up putting into practice something completely different from what they expect. Socialism seemed the only way to go, the question was how slow or fast?

Long-run speculation can undermine the immediate good we can do. Those who are 'practical,' 'sensible,' and 'realistic' hate speculations on general principles. If one relies too much on generous benefactors, one can lose respect in the eyes of those who spread their ideas as someone who has sold out. If one pretends to a final unquestioning view, that will only antagonize intellectuals. It can be that once we gain freedom, we take it for granted. We need a liberal utopia to inspire people "to work for an ideal, however small may be the prospects of its early realization." (Hayek F. , The Intellectuals and Socialism, 1949/1967) Free trade and freedom of opportunity may still move people, while 'reasonable freedom of trade' or 'relaxation of controls' may not.

> Unless we can make the philosophical foundations of a free society once more a living intellectual issue, and its implementation a task which challenges the ingenuity and imagination of our liveliest minds, the prospects of freedom are indeed dark. (Hayek F. , 1949/1967, p. 194)

The Mont Pelerin Society was created on April 10th, 1947 at a conference organized by Friederich Hayek. Members included Karl Popper, Ludwig von Mises, Milton Friedman and eventually Gary Becker. Membership is by invitation only. Popper thought open discussions would detect and correct possible errors if socialists were included, because of falsification by negative hypothesis, a standard first step in scientific methodology. Mises was not so tolerant. His vision of consumption as a democratic act and the marketplace as a forum for expression was an inspiration (Jones, 2012, p. 83). Daniel Stedman Jones describes policy institutes run by ideological entrepreneurs who …

> hustled to establish a media presence by raising their profile among sympathetic journalists, and to secure financial robustness for their organizations, and they fought for influence in the political process through the powerful promotion of markets. (Jones, 2012, p. 135)

Think tanks are nodes within an international network. The context was inhospitable and skeptical, but when the time came that the atmosphere shifted and politicians and public servants were looking for innovative ideas, the Neoliberal Thought Collective was already there waiting. They had been waging a war against overwhelming odds. Despite being ridiculed, they worked tirelessly to ensure free markets had a voice. It was a fight for the survival of individual freedom against the dominant hegemony of Keynesian socialism. It must have felt like banging one's head against the wall. The early think tanks had to keep faith, speculate and propose policy alternatives, and be prepared for when they finally had an opportunity.

Philip Mirowski described the MPS as:

> The main reason the MPS should serve as our talisman in tracking neoliberalism is because it exists as part of a rather special structure of intellectual discourse, perhaps unprecedented in the 1940s, one I would venture to propose to think of as a "Russian doll" approach to the integration of research and praxis in the modern world. ... I will use the term "thought collective" to refer to this multilevel, multiphase, multisector approach to the building of political capacity to incubate, critique, and promulgate ideas. ... Outsiders would rarely perceive the extent to which individual protagonists embedded in a particular shell served multiple roles, or the strength and pervasiveness of network ties, since they could never see beyond the immediate shell doll right before their noses. ... The Russian doll structure of the Neoliberal Thought collective would tend to amplify and distribute the voice of any one member throughout a series of seemingly different organizations,

> personas, and broadcast settings, lending it
> resonance and gravitas, not to mention fronting an
> echo chamber for ideas right at the time when
> hearing them was most propitious. (Mirowski,
> 2013, p. 43 & 46 & 49)

Mirowski argues that concentric from the MPS, which is international, are the academic departments dominated by neoliberal intellectuals, the foundations that fund conservative research, think tanks with quick and timely talking-points for friendly politicians, and talking heads for television news shows and opinion periodicals to show and convince the end consumers. With many of the same people filling separate roles. It is a very tight network. The network includes capitalists, various academic departments, foundations, international think tanks, journals, politicians, and single issue campaigns that appear to be spontaneous organizations. The loose coupling makes conspiracy deniable.

A History of the Ideologies of the Welfare State

In Canada there are three think tanks with direct relations to the Mont Pelerin Society: the Fraser Institute, the Atlantic Institute for Market Studies (AIMS), and the Macdonald-Laurier Institute (MLI) (Plehwe, Dieter and Walpen, Bernard, 2006) (Gutstein, 2014). There are eleven members of the MPS in Canada, including Tom Flanagan. The Fraser Institute was created by inviting Anthony Fisher, in 1975, to be the Co-Director of the Institute for Economic Affairs (IEA) with businessman Pat Boyle. Fisher took care of the fundraising and let Michael Walker do the intellectual output (Cockett, 1994). IEA was the model for many think tanks in America, often by Fisher himself; then after the 1980s around the world. Fisher was a tireless campaigner, fundraiser, and organizer who offered funding and resources for academic studies that the universities did not support. He set up the Atlas Foundation, an international umbrella organization for think tanks, and already in 1978 the Adam Smith Institute (ASI) was ...

> building a computerized file of individuals and organizations working to further the free society, and eventually it will be possible for other groups and individuals to obtain details of their co-workers on the basis of specialty, availability and many other useful items of information. (Butler as quoted in (Jones, 2012, p. 166))

One of the products from the invasion of the think tanks is the term 'junk science.' According to Mirowski (2011), accusations of 'junk science' degrade the quality of science both directly, by elevating dubious knowledge to comparable status as long-standing academic disciplines, and indirectly, by weakening the status of these disciplines by accusing them of dodgy corruption in their journals and the media. In the 1990s a few industries were fed up with the way academic science was being used in liability suits against them and decided to fund friendlier advocacy research. Think tanks promote otherwise isolated spokespersons that argue for the industry's side, laundering information through third party fronts, and moving debate away from science that seems impossible to challenge. Their job is to sow doubt.

> A whole mirror world of white papers and dubious fact sheets and counterfeit journal publications explicitly constructed to mimic academic scientific output while keeping the original funding and motivations obscure. (Mirowski, 2011, p. 299)

Scientists are prostitutes who can block or postpone unwanted regulation and stop liability settlements. Daubert v. Merrell Drew (1993) allows defendants to ask for the terms of 'sound science' to be settled in pre-trial, enabling the rich to buy time by challenging the quality of the science of an opponent. The Shelby Amendment to the Data Quality Act (1998) enables citizens to check whether federally funded research is 'sound science' by asking for all 'raw data' and 'notes,' thereby harassing and challenging any academic scientist one choses. It is to

134

prosecute political disputes as if they were scientific controversies, thereby leaving science compromised.

In the meantime, according to Mirowski (2011), people are getting measurably dumber and less willing to be engaged with novel complex arguments. This is not the naïve state of non-knowledge as in a 'vacuum,' nor selective attention due to fundamental limitations in our cognition, as in 'bounded rationality.' When the uneducated are reassured the truth is whatever they want it to be, and the asymmetric distribution of knowledge is seen as the result of choosing to optimize time and energy, there is the 'production of ignorance.' Hayek had a low opinion of intellectuals and deliberation. The market was a superior information processor. True rational thought occurs beyond and between people. It is because of the acknowledgement of our possible ignorance that we should leave the decision to a process we do not control. Knowledge is dispersed, incomplete and often contradictory, shared between separate individuals. According to Hayek the co-ordination of individuals in a complex society has to account for facts no one can survey; the only alternative is to be subject to the arbitrary control of men. 'Civilization' is when the individual in pursuit of their ends can profit from more knowledge than they possess. Unanticipated and unintended consequences can promote the public interest, so ignorance might guarantee the 'greater good' is served. "The think tanks/universities will churn out knowledge that elites want and need, perhaps even before they fully realize it; when elites see evidence of the right stuff, they will gladly pony up the funds to support it." (Mirowski, 2011, p. 326) It is a closed elite phenomenon with economic elites funding elite scientists but leaving everyone else ignorant. Only the Market can decide how knowledge should be 'subsidized, sorted, winnowed, and allocated.' The market actor is subservient to the Market in that they profit from knowledge they do not possess.

Paid experts should be apologists for those that hire them, as rational self-interest. Market intellectuals are blind to possible conflicts of interests. What will stand in the way will be that some think science serves a higher purpose, can speak truth to power, or rationally plan and execute 'social goals.' Intellectuals were disparaged as 'second-hand dealers in ideas.' Neoliberals value 'spontaneous order,' but revert to constructing order to achieve intentional ends when actually organizing something. This involves a double standard of truth, one for the insiders and another for the masses. The economist is supposed to stand above the economy and look down on its agents, to engage in self-reflection and decide whether to accept the terms and conditions of the model. The agent cannot rebel or change their values through deliberation. The economist either makes the agent dumber than they are, or cannot comment on the quality of knowledge. To see whether economics actually does the job it is supposed to is something left undone by economics.

Knowledge is expensive to produce but cheap to distribute. It requires an infinite patent period. Economists might argue litigation science is not harmful because it maximizes the competition between different points of view. But, shifting the image of education from 'preparation for citizenship' to personal 'human capital' shifts support from 'scholarships' to 'student loans.' The more the university becomes embroiled in market activities the more it loses political support while the privatization of research fences off free access to knowledge. All this while the economics profession has grown unchecked. Universities have boards of trustees composed of business men who will not seek humanists to commercialize the university. "Conflicts of interest are

138

pervasive and inevitable wherever or whenever research is fully privatized, because making money is never comprehensively isomorphic to making truth." (Cook et al as quoted by (Mirowski, 2011, p. 346) Neoliberalism may say making money is the only truth, and the only truth societies will absorb is the truth for which they are willing to pay. But conflicts of interests, according to Mirowski, is an institutional problem not a personal matter of ethics. "It is the story of the paladins of the economics' profession preaching the commercialization of science, profiting from its installment, all the while denying any of its unsavory aspects." (Mirowski, 2011, p. 349)

One application for the 'marketplace of ideas' has been opposition to the idea of global warming, or climate denial.

Humans can never be trusted to know whether the biosphere is in crisis or not, because both nature and society are dauntingly complex and evolving; therefore, the neoliberal solution is to enlist the

> strong state to allow the market to find its own way to the ultimate solution. (Mirowski, 2013, p. 336)

A broad spectrum of different policy responses for different time periods (short, mid-term, and long range) appear to come from distinctly different quarters but are in fact actually integrated to eventually capitulate to the market. When deployed in tandem, the net consequence is to leave the problem to be solved by the market, not the state.

'Science denialism' is a short-term measure to stomp out any impulses to respond and to buy time for commercial interests to construct market solutions to global warming. The first line of defence for complaints against the market is to blow smoke. Anyone should speak any falsehood they wish because the final judge of truth is the market, not scientific 'experts.' If it helps commercial propaganda in the interests of oil companies, so much the better.

140

'Carbon permit trading' is a mid-term strategy. The solution to any market failure is more markets. Political actors who are originally intent in using the state to curb emissions get diverted into arguing about permits, while emissions continue to grow. Trading carbon emissions was never supposed to work anyway. Lobbying and financial innovation will flood the market with excess 'permits, offsets, and other instruments' but never stunt the growth of emissions. According to Mirowski, trading systems reinforce oligopoly, it grandfathers in the largest emitters and penalizes new entrants, stifling technological measures to curb emissions.

'Geoengineering' is a long-term strategy. One far-out option is to inject particles into the stratosphere. No talk of whether it might be dangerous and ill-conceived. It is not about saving the planet but attempting to have a claim on privatizing the global troposphere. It is science fiction where entrepreneurs will always innovate market solutions to serious problems. The objective is to get an idea into general political discourse as a serious option. It diverts attention to Band-Aids while the patient is dying. Geoengineering just treats symptoms of global warming without curtailing emissions. Neoliberals have to capture the state to convince people something is being done while nothing really is. In Canada the green debate has been centered on the Keystone pipeline. Knowledge has been corrupted because the oil companies can afford their own science; has the issue become one of erring on the side of economic interests or on the side of caution?

Milton Friedman and Canadian Monetarism (1963)

Milton Friedman was the first to break through with neoliberal politics in a big way. He was the first to grab everyone's attention and upset Keynes' hegemony, though people later came to recognize Hayek as the more profound thinker. Keynes thought the depression was

142

caused by a collapse of effective demand for capital investment, and only direct spending by government could reverse the tide. The end of all policy was 'full employment' so there would not be a glut of overproduced and under-consumed goods. In *The Great Contraction 1929-1933* (1963) Milton Friedman showed the problem really was a shortening in the quantity of money in circulation. This led to bank failures and in turn led to runs on banks, which in turn shortened the money supply, and so on in a downward spiral. The Federal Reserve could have prevented the decline in the quantity of money and produce an increase, but they didn't. They made it worse because of a power struggle between the Washington and New York Federal Reserves along with some anti-Semitism against the NYFR. The depression was produced by government mismanagement, not instability in the private economy.

Later, the Philips curve suggested there was a trade-off between inflation and unemployment. Inflation was all right for Keynes, if it meant full employment. Friedman suggested in his Nobel Prize acceptance speech (1976) that we were experiencing stagflation where both inflation and unemployment rose at the same time. John Lucas came up with 'Rational Expectations' where the future was assumed to be like the past. If people expect inflation they will account for it when coordinating their plans. Any attempt to fool economic agents will be expected and counteracted in asking for higher wages. Unfortunately, higher wages further increased unemployment, and the government had to print more money to meet its obligations without borrowing or taxing, thereby aggravating the inflation. This way increasing the nominal wages ends up reducing and undermining real wages over time.

Government intervention can't improve macroeconomic performance; the economy will rapidly adjust returning quickly to natural equilibrium. There is a 'natural' rate of unemployment. Cutting back the money supply would create high unemployment, but there was going to be high unemployment anyway. So instead of aiming for 'full employment,' we should stop inflation through a mechanically steady increase in the money supply by 3% to 5% annually. In the end, governments really can't fool people. And in competitive markets, participants are supposed to be perfectly rational and display high levels of foresight. It is hard to see any beneficial role for government to intervene.

Harry Johnson, an eminent Canadian Keynesian known for his work on international exchange rates, retorted that ...

> A model should be a model – i.e., should try and incorporate the main relationships at work, not

> simply one dominated or allegedly dominant
> relationship supplemented with causal remarks. ...
> What annoys us all about this, I think, is your habit
> of insisting that the simplest possible models of
> each type should be tested against each other in
> this fashion, whereas the rest of us (especially the
> empirically inclined, now) take the view that if we
> need to construct more complex relationships to
> explain reality better, that is what we should do.
> (Johnson to Friedman 1965 as quoted in (Jones,
> 2012, p. 210)

He may as well have accused the Philips curve of

oversimplifying Keynes through neoclassical economic

math, by modeling it after hydraulics: 'priming the pump'

and 'push-pull', thereby making it a straw-man easy to

defeat, a technical detail contingently overturning the

reigning paradigm. Milton's critical analysis was still based

on the general foundations of Keynesian theory, having

been a Keynesian himself for many years. Besides, the

complaint that Keynes was inflationary originated when he

published his General Theory in 1936 and was mentioned

by Hayek in 1944 *The Road to Serfdom*. It was not news.

146

*

In the early 80's all three political figures seemed a natural trilogy: Ronald Reagan, Margaret Thatcher, and Brian Mulroney. Mulroney did not do so well in popularizing the neoliberal agenda. He was dubbed by journalists to be 'Robin Hood in reverse' giving tax breaks to the rich while cutting social programs for the poor, justified as preventing 'capital flight' in a global economy; a race to the bottom. At the leader's debate, Mulroney said 'read my lips, no free trade.' After he got in, he immediately arranged for NAFTA. It was a dramatic faux pas by a seemingly cynical and dishonest politician. People did not trust him after that, and hatred grew. The United Auto Workers (UAW) of Canada have never recovered from lost jobs and lower pay.

With NAFTA many complained that Canadian interests, such as generic drugs, were being sacrificed for American ones, like intellectual property rights with patents of longer life. (McQuaig, 1991) Pharmaceuticals have been the biggest drain on Medicare (Marchildon, 2010). As Linda McQuaig (1991) explained, interest shifted from securing access to the US market, which Congress and the Senate would not allow, to restraining the ability of the Canadian government to control its economy, as subsidies would be penalized. This shifted power from democracy, and the Canadian public's control over their own living conditions, to the private interests of internationals, backed by sanctions imposed by the American government. Canada was not allowed to impose any 'performance requirements,' such as locating in Canada or hiring Canadian workers. In 1984 there were 61 crown corporations; with privatization he sold 23, including Air Canada in 1989 and eventually Petro-Canada. He deregulated banks enough to allow them to sell insurance, giving special treatment to his friend Jim Robinson at American Express, who was so influential behind the trade talks. Amex could then sell insurance on their credit cards.

To top it all because John Crow was the governor of the Bank of Canada from 1987 to 1994, there was the policy of having double digit interest rates to kill inflation. Crow thought we should forget about full employment and have a zero tolerance policy for inflation, a prospect with diminishing marginal utility. Even Milton Friedman did not promote zero tolerance; he suggested a steady growth of the money supply by 3% a year. High interest rates would stop inflation, but they also added to the debt. They hurt borrowers and benefit lenders, such as those who speculated in currencies and bonds which did nothing to improve economic production - a form of high stakes gambling. High interest rates lowered the amount businesses borrowed to invest in plants and growing personnel, which led to a recession in the early 90s with a high rate of unemployment. This lowered income tax revenue while increasing the burden on unemployment insurance.

All of this added to the deficit, which think tanks were misleadingly complaining was the result of overspending on social programs that needed to be cut back. Commentators were saying we were 'living beyond our means,' while the real culprit, high interest rates, was left undiscussed. Not to mention, the interest rates encouraged foreign investment in the Canadian dollar, which drove its value up leaving Canadian products at a disadvantage as exports, exacerbating the recession. There is no estimating the extent to which the lack of investment hurt Canada's future. The loss of jobs was justified as lowering the wage demands and the resulting prices that led to inflation. (Prices would also have to drop to levels the unemployed could afford.) With reduced social programs such as 'unemployment insurance' people were more desperate for work and thereby more 'flexible.' No longer would workers be tolerated as 'lazy, spoiled, coddled, or inefficient free riders.' Globalization meant they would have to compete on the international stage against workers from third world countries who were willing to work for lower pay and fewer benefits.

In June 1993, Vincent Truglia, senior analyst specializing in Canada for Moody's Investor Services, one of the two biggest debt rating agencies in the world, said of Canada's debt: "Moody's sees no significantly negative trends in the Federal or public-sector debt outlooks which would justify changing the AAA ratings on $CDN debt of the Government of Canada." (Truglia as quoted in (McQuaig, 1995, p. 45)) AAA was Moody's highest rating. Truglia complained that Canada's debt crisis was highly exaggerated by using dodgy math. He was tired of people questioning his assessment.

> Several recently published reports have grossly exaggerated Canada's fiscal debt position. Some of

them have double counted numbers, while others have made inappropriate international comparisons, e.g. comparing Canadian gross debt to other countries' net debt. These inaccurate measurements may have played a role in exaggerated evaluations of the severity of Canada's debt problems. (Truglia as quoted in (McQuaig, 1995, p. 46)

The real problem Canada had with debt was its high interest rates. The Canadian financial sector was not pleased with Moody's report, which was using the debt crisis to justify cutting back popular social programs as a necessity. "One Canadian ... from a very large financial institution called me up on the phone screaming at me, literally screaming at me." (Truglia as quoted in (McQuaig, 1995, p. 44)) Once Canadians realized the hoax had been orchestrated by corporate think tanks it was too late; budget cuts had already been locked in and social programs were radically eroded. They have never recovered despite budget surpluses. Mulroney also came up with the GST which was hugely unpopular, because it

152

shifted the tax burden from companies to consumers. Increasing the tax load of the middle class led many citizens to resent their tax burdens and call for reduced government spending, furthering the cycle.

Mulroney's Meech Lake and Charlestown Accords ended up as constitutional disasters. After all was said and done, Kim Campbell was left holding the bag as a patsy. Only three PC members were returned in the next election. The first attempt at neoliberalism did not work out well; Mulroney was so hated he had decimated the Conservative Party.

New parties came out of the woodwork, like the Natural Law Party led by the magician Doug Henning. Two were quite strong, the Bloc and Reform. The Bloc were Quebec separatists inspired by the constitutional failures. While Reform was a new populism initiated in Alberta that railed against the out-of-touch elites of centralized planning with their strict and secretive party discipline.

A History of the Ideologies of the Welfare State

They campaigned against what they called a 'democratic deficit' that should be countered with referendums, initiatives, and recalls, as well as free votes in the House of Commons. It was as much a reaction against the way the Mulroney government imposed its agenda against the protests of the people, as it was against the high-handed authoritarian attitude of Pierre Trudeau who imposed the National Energy Program (NEP) in the 1970s that decimated Alberta's oil economy. It assumed people wanted to pay lower taxes and reduce the culture of dependency that welfare created. Putting people back to work, as programs in 'labour market activation,' however, could be helpful or punitive depending on the law or program and its intent (Kenworthy, 2010).

In November 1993 Jean Chretien became Prime Minister. He retired John Crow in February 1994 and let interest rates float, much to the relief of mortgage owners. In 1995 shared-cost programs were replaced with a single

154

block transfer, the Canada Health and Social Transfer (CHST), lumping together the funding of Health Care, Social Assistance, and Post-Secondary Education. It gave provinces more room to shift spending from unpopular welfare programs to more popular ones like Health Care and Education. It also had an amount and a limit beyond which there was no remuneration. In 1996, a 15% cut in transfer payments eliminated the Federal deficit, leaving it up to the provinces to make up the shortfall. The rationale was said to be merely eliminating the deficit, not reducing social programs, though the result was the same. Mulroney had said he wanted to eliminate the deficit, but he was too busy cutting taxes for the rich and stopping inflation with high interest rates that added to the debt. Chretien had campaigned with Keynesian rhetoric about the need for full employment but, in the end, he was afraid of the threat of capital flight, deindustrialization and downsizing. He thought we could not really reach full employment again. He did, however, refuse banking deregulation and bank mergers. In 2004, under Steven Harper, the CHST divided into the Canada Health Transfer and the Canada Social Transfer for more transparency.

In 2008 there was an international stock market crash caused by some shady dealings in American housing securities. Alan Greenspan, thirteenth chairman of the Federal Reserve from 1987 to 2006, believed in deregulation and Ayn Rand. His answer to any little slowdown in the American markets was to lower interest rates thereby heating them up again. He did that through many bubbles over forty years, until he discovered 'a flaw' that ended in the 2008 crash. Tim Geithner, Ben Bernanke and Hank Paulson's answer to the crash was TARP, $72 billion of capital injections as a bailout for the banks, without any guarantees from the governors. The last two independent investment banks left standing had to take advantage of the Federal Open Window. It was the end of the era of independent investment banking, the banks were practically nationalized. Ben Bernanke was the chairman of the Federal Reserve and Henry Paulson was the Secretary of the Treasury. Timothy Geithner, a fan of Milton Friedman, was president of Federal Reserve Bank of New York. His intellectual expertise was in the Great Depression. He knew the best way to turn a recession into a depression was to shorten the money supply with high interest rates, so they threw money at the problem hoping to mop it up later, hoping it would all go away while doing nothing to punish those whose reckless behaviour led to the crash in the first place. Maybe the banks should have been officially nationalized.

When the crash happened Mark Carney, Harper's finance minister, took over the Bank of Canada and lowered all interest rates to their lowest levels and sat on them for a year. It was a bold move that kept Canada from the worst effects of the crash. He was a Canadian hero who went on to chair the Bank of England until Brexit. Government rescue packages in Canada after the 2008 crash were 22% of GDP and 361 USD billions (Buckley, 2011, p. 270). Greenspan lowered interest rates when markets slowed down thereby heating up bubbles, where Carney lowered interest rates to fend off a depression. The same action with different consequences in different situations. Wasn't more information needed than just the price, to make the right decision here? Contra Hayek.

*

Milton Friedman was a policy specialist. His most famous proposal for the income contingent loan program (ICLP) was written in 1955 as the essay 'The Government and Education,' though he first mentioned it in 1945. A user fee would shift financing from government grants to student loans. Rather than a subsidy, where the student bore no cost, from the general government pot where all is paid by the taxpayer, the student should bear all cost,

158

and reap all rewards, from investing in their own human capital. The problem is to make capital available. "They should not be prevented by market imperfections from making the investment when they are willing to bear all the costs." (Friedman, Capitalism and Freedom, 1962, p. 105) The argument is since students are the ones who benefit from university, they should be paying the cost, not the taxpayer.

It is a way of privatizing the public debt. The burden would be shifted from the past generation (who benefited from lower rates) to the present generation. The old system made students pay a set rate regardless of income and had forced a number of them into bankruptcies and defaults. The ICLP would not demand payment until the graduate is earning a high enough salary, though the interest will still accumulate. But the payments can be so low they don't qualify for bankruptcy. There will be exceptions for special needs and single mothers, for whom the paying students would make up the difference.

The loans can be given from the federal government to the students directly and they spend it on the university they choose. This will increase consumer and federal control, making sure the money is spent on a good education. The institutions will be forced to compete for funding, making their programs more competitive, catering to the desires of consumers.

The banks also gain more control over repayment. Students will pay back regularly on schedule rather than diffusely over a lifetime through taxes. It can be within the bank's power to refuse loans for those enrolled in high risk programs like the arts and humanities.

As funding shifts from government to the consumer, tuition fees can rise to full cost. The Globe and Mail congratulated Queen's and the University of

Toronto's executive training program for just these measures, saying it made them truly autonomous and independent from government patronage and control. Students afraid of the cost should be encouraged to go elsewhere.

> Advocates of ICLP see such contributions – an informed political citizenry, guardians of Canada's heritage, a population with intellectual horizons that lead to more mature use of leisure time – only as externalities and not to be taken into the equation. (As quoted in (Emberley, 1996, p. 180)

In America, what happens if you can't repay a student loan?

> "You will be hounded for life," he warns. "They will garnish your wages. They will intercept your tax refunds. You become ineligible for federal employment." He adds that any professional licence can be revoked and Social Security checks docked when you retire. (As quoted in (Mirowski, 2013, p. 138))

*

Another one of Friedman's policy innovations was the negative income tax (NIT), a tax credit for the working poor. Jane Jenson (2010) explained it was first used in Canada with the 1966 guaranteed income supplement (GIS). In 1966 incomes of families with dependent children experimented with the NIT, later it became part of child benefits. Benefits were subject to income testing, so were no longer a universal right. In 1975 'an income tested spouse's allowance was added to OAS/GIS to cover those, usually women, between age sixty and sixty-four whose spouse received the minimum benefit and they themselves had no earned income,' later extended to widows and widowers. In 1989 means testing replaced universal Old Age Security (OAS). Optimism about the effects of the negative income tax may have been responsible for a lack of direct investing by the government in such things as day cares and preschools, for which Canada has been lagging behind world standards (OECD data quoted by (Bradshaw, Johnathan and Finch, Naomi, 2010, p. 468).

In Canada 2010, there was increasing concern about investing in the human capital of children and adapting to market conditions that demand job flexibility, with part-time, temporary, or self-employment service jobs. Employment Insurance (EI) is harder to get, forcing a return to the workforce because of a lack of alternative income, an exception being those with disabilities. Adults with children have access to benefits and services others do not. Milton's darling the 'negative income tax,' however, only supplements low-income earners so parents can stay at work, and do nothing to help the most vulnerable class whose income is so low they do not pay taxes, such as those on fixed incomes who cannot work. The Canada Child Tax Benefit (CCTB) is income tested on a sliding scale, while The National Child Benefit Supplement

(NCBS) goes to low-income families; both reach middle and low classes. Unfortunately, they have done little to reduce child poverty. Canada has lagged behind the world in high-quality preschool and child care (OECD data quoted by Bradshaw & Finch 2010, p.468). Preference for the negative income tax has undermined direct investment in these services.

The Austrian Libertarian Ludwig von Mises (1949)

Friedman was not without his critics. In the 1920s both Ludwig von Mises and Friederich Hayek saw the American boom as unstable and predicted the depression when no one else did. The Austrian theory of the business cycle holds booms are created by the low interest rates of central banks. Friedman thought the Great Depression was caused by shortening the money supply, while Mises saw the problem as low interest rates creating an artificial and unsustainable boom that necessarily had to be readjusted.

164

To stop inflations and recessions Mises thought we should
be on a gold standard which does not allow the
government to depreciate the dollar by creating more
money. This effectively ties the hands of the state.
Friedman thought gold was unnecessarily costly to mine;
we should instead curb arbitrary authority by having a rule
of increasing the money supply by three to five percent
per year. Mises thought this gave too much discretion to
the government. Libertarianism is not neoliberalism. His
solution seemed unpalatable, however, during the
depression because it would have meant higher
unemployment.

Mises was particularly critical of Keynes' call for
easy money to help curb unemployment and promote
investment; he preferred a 'sound money' policy.
Government can only subsidize increased expenditures by
raising taxes which is unpopular, borrowing and getting
further into debt, or by printing money and creating

inflation. Inflation is not a trade-off for higher employment, but only makes matters worse. It lowers the value of the poor's fixed income thereby lowering consumer demand while creating further unemployment down the line because of high wages. It benefits borrowers only in the short run at the expense of hurting creditor's investments in the long run. It was thought workers will not resent an inflation they can't see more than a cut in wages.

Murray Rothbard a follower of Mises drafted a book on *America's Great Depression* in 1963 popularizing the Austrian theory at the same time Friedman published *A Monetary History of the United States* (1962). Rothbard also wrote a huge economic tome *Man, Economy, and State* (1962) based directly on Mises' magnum opus *Human Action: A Treatise on Economics* (1949). Mises based his economics on what he called catallactics, the subjective but unavoidable logic of practical choice.

166

Rothbard (2002) thought this did not defend economic rights as effectively as could be done under the protection of natural law. In contrast to Rothbard who preferred individuals to purchase their services from private protection agencies, Robert Nozick (1974) was inspired to imagine backing into a night watchman state (army, police and courts to protect society against fraud, theft and violence) in trying to not to violate anyone's rights to justly acquire or freely transfer property. In the end libertarianism has never formed a national party that could compete with the Republicans or Democrats, and never found a following in Canada. While neoliberalism has influenced both parties.

Summary

We can see George Grant lamented for Canadian sovereignty, which was lost by the liberalization of Canada through free trade. He was from a tradition that was ending, of a Red Tory where the common good should restrain greed and promote Canadian nationalism.

Hayek and Friedman represented the neoliberal resistance to the welfare state. Hayek created an international network through the Mont Pelerin Society of think tanks that would be ready with policy recommendations, for when the Keynesian hegemony toppled. Eventually it did thanks to the work of Milton Friedman, who was more directly relevant with his policy recommendations. He showed Keynes was wrong about the depression - it was not caused by a shortage of demand for consumer goods but by a shortening the monetary supply with high interest rates.

In 1976 Friedman argued that in a stagflation where unemployment and inflation were going up at the same time, there was not much that could be done about unemployment since it was close to the 'natural rate' anyway, therefore we should try to worry about stopping

168

inflation by increasing the money supply by only 3% annually. He shifted policy from seeking full employment and toppled Keynes.

Friedman had a lot of influence in Canadian politics, shifting it to a neoliberal agenda; using the deficit as the excuse to cut our social programs, because we were 'living beyond our means,' when really the debt was the result of a policy of high interest rates causing a recession. In the end they were not able to eliminate the welfare state, only cut it back a little.

3: Social Investment vs. Social Insurance

Before the Seventies, T. H. Marshall and Tom Bottomore wrote *Citizenship and Social Class* (1950) where they argued that starting with legal rights we progressed on to political rights. It was only natural we would follow with the economic rights of the welfare state. But by 1956, C. A. R. Crosland had written *The Future of Socialism* where he argued the Fabian Society should give up on nationalization and collective ownership, the true goal was equality. Education should not be a steep narrow staircase but a wide easy lift. Promoting widespread education is a means towards equalizing resources. The socialists themselves had already narrowed their agenda from communism to market friendly socialism.

Yet, it seems impossible to eliminate the welfare state, it is too popular. It is here to stay, but there are now two different justifications for it that can conflict. One is the theory of 'human capital' by the neoliberal Gary Becker, where we create a more productive work force by investing in health and education. This inspired the idea of 'social investment' by Anthony Giddens where the state is to financially help us through periods of transition. We need to take on more risk, not avoid it. Universal social services are no longer considered a citizen's right. They have become means-tested so that only the poorest are eligible. The alternative, which is much older, is to say that we face certain risks in modern society, and we should have social insurance to protect ourselves from them. This is supposed to include everyone. The welfare state is supposed to be the economic rights of a citizen. Thus, we have the contrast of social investment vs. social insurance. It might be good to pursue both, but they are different rationales that can diverge and conflict.

I. Social Investment: Neoliberalism for the Left

Gary Becker and Human Capital (1964)

Gary Becker saw there were different forms of investment in human capital; such as on-the-job training, schooling, gathering information about economic opportunities, as well as physical and emotional health. Training might lower current receipts and raise current expenditures profitably if future receipts are sufficiently raised or future costs sufficiently lowered. Costs and returns are to be borne by the employee who would see their employment opportunity advance. They pay for it by receiving lower wages now for opportunities for higher earnings later. The steeper the curve, the greater the cost and greater the return. The more concave, the more important to make the investment at a younger rather than an older age.

172

If the firm pays for all training there would be too many applicants. If they don't pay skilled labour enough they will not meet their needs for personnel. On-the-job training is mixed between general and specialized knowledge. General knowledge can benefit many firms other than the initial investor, while specialized knowledge is specific to the firm and benefit only the investor. Firms tend not to invest in general knowledge because they lose on the investment if the employee is hired away.

Specialized knowledge includes familiarizing new employees with their organizations. This should also include employment agency fees, job searching, and time 'interviewing, testing, checking references, and bookkeeping.' After hiring costs, firms know only a little about their new employees. So investment takes the form of 'testing, rotation among departments, trial and error.' Firms don't pay any of the general cost, and only some of the specific costs. Rational firms pay 'generally trained' employees the same, and specifically trained employees a higher wage than they can get elsewhere. Because specific training is done more by the employee, age-earning profiles are steeper and more concave. Specifically, trained workers are less likely to be unemployed, and they receive higher wages. Both the quit and layoff rates would be low and fluctuate less.

Firms collect larger profits from higher productivity. The willingness of firms or employees to pay for specific training depends on labour turnover. A firm is hurt by losing an employee and an employee is hurt by losing a job. This can be offset by offering employees some of the return from training. Pension plans can insure against losing employees. Shifting costs to employees as well as returns will bring supply more in line with demand. The share of each, the firm and the employee, depend on quitting and layoff rates, which in turn is affected by risk and liquidity preferences.

Education is an investment in human capital for a longer term payoff. Schools specialize in the production of training. Some types of knowledge are mastered better if related to practical problems, others require prolonged specialization. A student can't earn as much as they would otherwise because they cannot work as much or regularly. Tuitions, fees, books and supplies, unusual transportation and lodgings are direct expenses. They steepen the age-earnings profile by lowering reported earnings during the investment period, raising them later on. Knowledge about economic opportunities such as enabling a person to buy the cheapest gear or get a better job can raise incomes. Investment in employment agencies and want-ads, talking to friends and visiting firms, time and resources in moving, earn a return in higher earnings than would otherwise be received. The larger the number of alternatives the lower the cost to the worker.

Lower earnings due to education are 'investment costs.' Higher earnings are 'investment returns.' Costs are related to returns by an 'internal rate of return.' Young people have a greater incentive to invest because they can collect the return over more years. Specialists have a greater incentive to invest in themselves. Human capital is a very illiquid asset - it cannot be sold. Therefore, it cannot be used as collateral, necessitating a sizable liquidity premium. The longer between investment and return, the less there is such knowledge available. "Young persons are supposed to be especially prone to overestimating their ability and chance of good fortune." (Becker, 1964, p. 41) The young are particularly liable to be ignorant of their abilities and investment opportunities.

Financing may be problematic because people cannot postpone their investment too long; age-profiles were steeper and more concave among more skilled and educated persons. "Instead of only benefitting from

176

activities by others, the average earner is made a prime mover of development through the investment in himself." (Becker, 1964, p. 45) Those with more ability are more likely to invest in themselves; they are more likely to migrate and continue their education. High earnings can signify both more ability and a better environment. However, college graduates earn more even without their education.

The amount invested is a function of the rate of return expected. Since abler persons will invest more, ability and investment are more strongly positively correlated, accounting for the skew in incomes, especially when abilities are more evenly distributed in the beginning. Income is determined more by the intangible asset of knowledge than the physical capital of the rich.

Investing in human capital also benefits the wider community. Isabela Mares (2010) explains that while it is expected higher taxes and spending on social programs can result in slower economic growth, empirical research has failed to confirm this. Instead investment in human capital has shown that investment in education can have positive effects on growth, as do investments in health and infrastructure. All accepted, as positive investments for governments, by the Washington consensus. People would rather see someone going to university than dependent on welfare. Social programs have provided positive externalities that outweigh the distortion of high taxes. Between 1870 and 1913 growth was 1.4 per cent and between 1913 and 1950 it was 1.2 percent. The period between 1950 and 1973, the rise of the welfare state, was 3.7 per cent, three times higher than previous periods. (Mares, 2010) Social insurance policies have given employees the incentive to invest long-term in industry- or firm-specific skills. Modest spending on health care has led to significant reductions in infectious diseases and malnutrition, along with declines in infant mortality and increases in life expectancy, which correspond to increased average productivity with fewer sick days. For unions, higher benefits in pensions, healthcare, or unemployment are the same as higher wages, so they can be more moderate in their demands. All positive externalities.

Anthony Giddens and The Social Investment State (1998)

Anthony Giddens took lessons from the neoliberals Hayek and Becker and applied them to Social Democracy as a third way between the old left and the new right. He took Social Democracy and remade it, putting a more humane face upon neoliberal thinking. After the cold war Socialism has had to make peace with markets and learn to live with them. He was friends with and advisor to Tony Blair, the head of the Independent Labour Party in England, and the US Democrat President Bill Clinton. Both were supposedly on the left but continued the neoliberal agenda anyway. In Canada the Liberal leader Jean Chretien preached Keynesian full employment but followed deficit reduction instead after he was elected. He was afraid of capital flight. Blair, in particular, spoke out against the welfare state in a way summarized by Ross:

> Social justice had been wrongly equated with equality of result, undermining personal responsibility and the work ethic; social justice had been wrongly equated with higher levels of public spending without the due consideration for economic and social trade-offs; social democracy had wrongly assumed that the state could compensate for market failures, resulting in bloated government and the suppression of individual goods and values; social democracy had wrongly promoted social rights without due consideration for responsibilities, producing a lack of reciprocity; and social democracy had wrongly dismissed the effectiveness of the market. (Ross as quoted in (King, Desmond and Ross, Fiona, 2010)

Giddens idea is the 'social investment state.' He thought risk and security should be shifted to create a society of responsible risk takers. People need protection when things go wrong, but more important material and moral capacities should be provided to help people move through major periods of transition.

A meritocratic society with high inequalities of outcome can threaten social cohesion. Someone only marginally more talented can command a much higher salary than another. Those at the bottom know they are there because of their lack of ability, which is only right and proper. Unfortunately, privileged groups may exclude themselves from society and pull out from public education and public health. While "in declining areas, housing falls into disrepair, and lack of job opportunities produces education disincentives, leading to social instability and disorganization." (Giddens, 1998, p. 104) Limiting voluntary exclusion at the top is needed to create a more inclusive society at the bottom. Welfare must not be targeted only to the poor. That only creates division and negative connotations. Instead the state should invest in helping people acquire skills and education as a redistribution of opportunities that contribute to society.

According to Giddens, the welfare state has been undemocratic. 'Old-boy networks, backstage deals, unashamed forms of patronage' were no longer acceptable. Welfare institutions could be 'bureaucratic, alienating, inefficient and have perverse consequences.' Benefits to counter unemployment can produce more unemployment. Expectations can become locked in with interest groups entrenched, so benefits cannot be reduced. This means social programs are not flexible.

We shouldn't only protect ourselves from risk, but harness the energetic side of risk to provide more opportunities. Active risk taking is an inherently entrepreneurial activity that benefits both society and the individual. Entrepreneurs often spot possibilities others miss. Giddens thought such benefits as pensions should be used as people wished, to leave work at any age, to finance education, or provide reduced working hours for raising children.

> Without the new ideas guaranteed by entrepreneurship there is the absence of competition. Entrepreneurship is a direct source of jobs. It also drives technological development, and gives people opportunities for self-employment in times of transition. (Giddens, 1998, p. 124)

Government policy can offer venture capital, as well as give some security when things go wrong.

> In the positive welfare society, the contract between individual and government shifts, since autonomy and the development of self – the medium of expanding individual responsibility – become the prime focus. (Giddens, 1998, p. 128)

Robert Putnam on Civil Society and Social Capital (2000)

Important alternatives to having the 'social investment state' delivering social services are the volunteers, foundations, and charities of civil society, which itself is neither wholly private industry nor public government. Giddens thinks we need to devolve power from a distant, uncaring and inefficient centralized authority to local initiatives. The state is intrusive, controlling, and dehumanizing. Civil society can offer alternatives to government services. Markets and states may not function well without citizens taking on more responsibility, but citizens also have to alter their expectations of the state. However, in taking on state functions, civil society may become more like the state. The role of a check on the state would be compromised if civil society supplanted or became a partner to the state. (Chambers, Simone and Kopstein, Jeffrey, 2006)

184

Robert Putnam (2000) argues that beyond physical capital (infrastructure) and human capital (health and education) there is social capital (trust and contacts, mutual self-help). Trust is an inherently social good that cannot be practiced alone. It lowers transaction costs by decreasing the need to police and enforce contracts. A person is more likely to contribute if they think everyone does the same. A person is more willing to pay their taxes if they feel few people free ride.

Putnam argued social networks provided advice, job leads, and letters of reference. Because our friends and family tend to know the same people and opportunities we do, our more casual acquaintances can lead us to unexpected opportunities. Support groups can help those with fewer financial and educational resources, providing child care and loans. Connectedness also preserves physical health against heart attacks, since isolation is stressful. Social support lessens the severity of depression and helps speed recovery.

Parents involved with their children's school and education have children less likely to do drugs, skip school, fight, or have teenage pregnancies. Mutual trust and altruism among neighbors, and a willingness to intervene when they see children misbehaving, is strongly correlated to a lack of crime. Places where people do not get involved in local organizations such as churches, or serve as role models, see more positive social capital replaced by gangs who offer similar social benefits. These gangs sell drugs but they also donate to charities and help control crime, important when resources such as cooperation between communities and police is lacking. But if the state is overly intrusive that undermines a citizen's competence to live up to civic responsibilities.

According to Simone Chambers and Jeffrey Kopstein (2006) liberal democracy depends on reproducing democratic virtues, such as tolerance, cooperation, and respect. It is to unite separate citizens to pursue the public good beyond private interests. In good civil society, people see those with whom they deeply disagree as deserving respect. Bad civil society promotes hatred and bigotry. They asked whether we should only support those groups who promoted civility, or would that undermine associational freedom?

Civil society is not something one can just throw money at and expect to work. International NGOs often take development out of the local's hands, taking charge and building for them. It takes time to develop strong civil associations from the ground up, and the local population must do it for themselves. Giddens (1998) argues that community building should use support networks and self-help to generate economic renewal in low-income neighborhoods. Injection of economic resources should support local initiatives, rather than their being dependent on benefits. Putnam (2000) argues that voluntary associations teach civic skills like giving a presentation or running a meeting. Unfortunately, civil society tends to favour the rich, educated, and well organized. Grass roots organizations have largely been replaced by letter networks with small professional staffs supported by donations. Not everyone has the time, energy, or inclination to get involved and do it themselves, so they just send money. Both the Right and the Left have made strong claims on civil society which it may find difficult to fulfill.

Anthony Giddens is willing to cut back on government services if they can be delivered by NGOs in civil society. However, one of the reasons for replacing charity with government services is to enforce universal standards rather than offering haphazard and uncoordinated philanthropy. The bonus for government services over private charity is that government can be

188

held accountable for how they deliver their services. Charity is purely voluntary and a gift cannot be so critiqued.

Ulrich Beck and *The Great Risk Shift* (2006)

The social investment state comes with a culture of risk. In *Risk Society* (1992) Ulrich Beck argues that because the new left opted for more personalized alternative lifestyles, people identify less and less with economic class, and this has weakened traditional support networks. Because of less job security and the increase in part-time, temporary, or self-employed work, individuals have to choose their next job as they would manage a resume portfolio. Biography has become open, to be constructed personally, but at the same time subject to external and internationally remote factors that are in themselves uncontrollable risks. Unemployment has been integrated into part of the employment system, and the boundary

A History of the Ideologies of the Welfare State

between formal and informal work has been eroded. Factory halls and tall office buildings have been replaced by outsourced mobile computers. Space and time have both become more flexible. As people's sovereignty over their work has increased, risk has been privatized. Social crises have come to appear as personal ones.

In *The Great Risk Shift* (2006) Jacob Hacker argues a calamity that can happen in a second can have devastating consequences that change a life forever. Social insurance is the idea that some risks can be effectively dealt with by spreading costs. In the name of 'personal responsibility' risk has shifted from corporations and governments to citizens and workers. "Employers want out of the social contract forged in the more stable economy of the past." (Hacker, 2006, p. 7) They have been getting what they want.

A thirty-year period of shared prosperity has given way to greater insecurity. It used to be thought the next

190

generation would be more stable and economically better off. No longer. Corporations used to offer pensions - they do so less often. The American dream has it that those who worked hard, made good choices, and did right by their families would prosper. Increased insecurity means the increased possibility of being laid off, losing health coverage, or having a serious illness happen to a family member, any one of which can involve costs that can plunge a family into poverty. Even the highly educated have been affected. Even people who are risk-averse have experienced wild income swings. Good decisions do not affect insecurity.

In an 'ownership society,' according to Hacker, people are encouraged to set up their own private accounts to deal with risks on their own, and money that would go into group insurance has been given to individuals to do with as they please. Advocates for the personal responsibility crusade worry social insurance promotes moral hazard, and call for privatizing social security. Moral hazard means that the more people are protected against risk, the less do they avoid risk. It is thought more efficient that those with a pre-existing condition or expected higher risk to pay more. Cushioning the consequences of bad behaviour only encourages more bad behaviour, they say.

Hacker argued things like tax breaks for RRSPs create a system parallel to government programs that have undermined their support. It is argued that if there is competition for savings either internally within the government or with private corporations, costs will be kept down on social programs and prisons, while competition promotes efficiency by giving clients a say in the services they are offered, such as with school vouchers. Government programs may even make money if they are more entrepreneurial and charge user fees.

192

Philip Mirowski (2013) criticizes the neoliberal unreserved embrace of risk. Risk is supposed to be the primary method of changing one's identity to live life to the fullest. Taking chances is seen as the proof one is engaged in the pursuit of self-advantage rather than accepting one's lot bequeathed by others. Since we are completely ignorant in the face of the all-knowing market, our utter subjection to the risk of the market is an act of giving oneself up to powers greater than ourselves. Instead of being protected by the welfare state like a drone, people are supposed to revel in the opportunities to remake themselves. Instead of seeing gambling as bilking the poor who cannot walk away, the person who abjectly submits to risk is to be hailed as a hero. The result is any economic transaction no matter how dangerous is seen as freely entered into by the entrepreneur and therefore non-coercive and free of exploitation. When things collapse, taking a risk means you brought the failure upon yourself, therefore the loss is perfectly justified. It was your choice. Still while people are supposed to be busy escaping their substantive selves, insurance firms still force people into actuarial categories like 'class, age, and sex.'

Michel Foucault and the Entrepreneur of the Self (1979/2008)

The society of risk affects how we see ourselves. Foucault was influenced by the communitarian theories of Martin Heidegger and Louis Althusser that both describe how an individual is forged from and by their group. In *Discipline and Punish* (1975) he describes the horror story of how individuals are created in a disciplinary society. The paranoia of being caught without knowing it, by being watched by those who cannot themselves be watched. The neoliberalism of Gary Becker and Friederich Hayek offered Foucault an alternative analysis such that we were

194

to be entrepreneurs of ourselves, not to be psychoanalyzed in depth but influenced through surface economic incentives, to be busy creating new markets.

Heidegger (Heidegger, 1962) said we do not begin by distinguishing ourselves from others. Individuation is something achieved. For life to be worthwhile we have to become authentic, not go along with the crowd. 'One' usually takes pleasure the way 'they' take pleasure. Dasein's possibilities are for others to dispose of as they please, the more effectively the more inconspicuously. The 'they' prescribe the way of interpreting the world which lies so close to us we tend to pass over it. Everything gets obscured because what is covered up is passed off as something familiar and accessible to everyone. It is always 'they' who did it, or in the end it was 'no one.' This can disburden Dasein, if one is inclined to take it easy. Feeling not at home, anxiety makes us peripherally aware of being lost in the crowd, with our conscience bringing us back to ourselves. Dasein is defined as an entity concerned with the question of its own being as a project, the quality of which is supposed to be authentic.

The structuralist Marxist Louis Althusser (1971), on the other hand, said people do not become self-conscious without the external pressure to behave properly. There is an ambiguity in the term subject. On the one hand, it refers to a center of initiatives that are responsible for its actions. On the other hand, it refers to a subjected being who submits to a higher authority and is stripped of all freedom except freely accepting submission. Individuals are addressed by ideology in order to transform them into subjects, free to obey or disobey but forced to respond.

A third form of being a subject, studied by Foucault, is as a university discipline. Foucault (1975) reveals how the masses are channeled and controlled through a one-way observation, where those who being watched cannot watch those who are watching them. The result is paranoia, with internalized coercion masquerading as a conscience. Thus, the social creation of the self, for Foucault, is a horror story. In discipline, the smallest infraction or failure to live up to standards can be penalized with repeating the same exercise until the child gets it right, or learns his lesson, creating docile and useful bodies with the least cost of displaying power. Knowledge is indispensable for discipline, which does not simply treat the population as a single uniform mass, but separates, analyzes, differentiates, and above all trains them. It studies and creates individuals as targets and instruments for its control. In relation to common behavior, the prisoner is differentiated and individualized. This creates an accumulation of formal documentation that is to be correlated and entered into the general register of a central office as a permanent record in a case file on the individual's history that is never closed and which can always be used to intervene in their life. Thus, the reality

A History of the Ideologies of the Welfare State

of individuality is constructed and imposed through the many minor techniques of coercion and observation that function in institutions. In this way power and knowledge are inextricably linked in a disciplinary society.

In *The Birth of Biopolitics: Lectures from the College de France 1978-1979* (2008b) Foucault said that one thing that is unique with neoliberalism is the way it uses economic theory to analyze noneconomic phenomena, not only to aid in understanding but to critique policy in terms of efficiency in the allocation of scarce resources. A good example is Public Choice, which applies economic analysis to voting behaviour.

Gary Becker advanced penal theory beyond the disciplinary society with its strict construction of the self by shifting the focus from eliminating all crime to tolerating a certain amount of crime that does not cost too much. There is a diminishing marginal utility to exterminating crime. Good penal policy does not try to

198

end all crime but seeks a balance between the supply of crime and its negative demand. Society does not have a limitless need for compliance and so does not need an exhaustive disciplinary system. The question becomes how much crime can we tolerate?

Instead of going after major suppliers and labs for illegal drugs, the police find it more profitable to go after street-corner dealers and their clients. The hardcore drug-user has an inelastic demand and is willing to do anything, such as mug and rob to supply their fix. Costs have to be kept low for them, while new users still have an elastic demand and should be discouraged from pursuing such drugs further.

No longer is the criminal to be psychoanalyzed, but treated as a rational maximizer with strict penalties. It is not the inside of a criminal that is the target but the economic environment, through punitive fines and incarceration. The way to correct errors is to make the fines and penalties too expensive to ignore, not probe into their psychology. The penal code does not give any substantive, qualitative, or moral definition of a crime. A crime is any act punishable by law. Becker shifted the perspective to that of the person committing a crime; it is whatever puts him at risk of being punished. It is anyone who invests in an action, expects a profit from it, and accepts the risk of a loss. This analysis of rational choice affects our self-image.

In the neoliberal analysis *homo economicus* is an entrepreneur of himself. He is his own capital, his own producer, and his own source of earnings. Health care and public hygiene are important investments that both improve human capital and also preserve it to be employed as long as possible. The ability to geographically relocate to a higher paying position is also important. It can temporarily lower wages and psychologically dislocate the person, until they have resettled, but it is an investment for higher status and remuneration. The same is true of education. An entrepreneur is someone who takes a chance to earn a profit and accepts the risk of a loss.

Foucault used genetics as an example of investing in human capital. Genetics enable us to tell which individuals are at risk of contracting a certain disease at some point in their life. This risk is the result of a particular pairing of parents. If one wants to have a child with a genetic makeup as good as oneself or better, one has to choose a mate whose genetic makeup is at least as good as one's own. To do that one has to invest in working hard enough for a good salary and status to attract someone with good genetic makeup, to produce a child with high human capital. If society took it upon itself to promote high human capital it may have to take over screening and controlling unions to eliminate certain diseases and defects. That is, if society wants to cultivate and improve genetic human capital.

Investments in human capital should create new kinds of markets where there were none. We should use human capital to provide technical improvements as well as training and education so the social framework can be modified, not so they directly affect markets, but so something like agriculture can function as a market. The question is how to modify the material, cultural, technical, and legal basis to promote markets where they don't already exist. The government should not protect society from the effects of the market, but should regulate society *by* the market. Social insurance should correspondingly be privatized. Intervention is called for to introduce competitive markets through legislation. According to Hayek, laws make markets possible and define them, they are not given as something natural. We are not stuck with a capitalism that has its own internal logic, but can invent a new one.

Hayek thought laws should intervene in a way that is purely general, not tied to a specific purpose. It should be the rules of the game, whose outcome is not predetermined by the arbitrary will of authorities and committees. The more people are freed from planning, as enterprises allowed to compete, the more friction there is to be worked out in impartial courts. The rule of law means normal courts can intercede between legislatures and individuals, to affect the creation and application of the law in a self-correcting manner. Laws can create an economy that regulates itself. 'Law and economics' is one of the new right-wing academic subjects inspired by Hayek.

Foucault went beyond Giddens in analyzing 'apparatuses of security.' Security gains in importance at the same time as individuals are called upon to regulate

A History of the Ideologies of the Welfare State

themselves. In *Security, Territory, Population* (1978/2008a) Foucault explained that apparatuses of security are a third kind of political technology, apart from legal systems and disciplinary mechanisms. These apparatuses involve tweaking the regulation of independent processes, not the abject subjugation to an oppressive sovereign will as in discipline. This entails a theory that cuts off the head of Hobbes' sovereign and moves beyond the Marxian/Freudian analytics of repression. In *The History of Sexuality Volume 1: An Introduction* (1976, p.94-95) Foucault had already speculated that relations of power were intentional in that they have strategies that aim at goals, but are not subjective in that there is no one who has invented them. They are not the result of a choice or decision. Also, they are productive for and not external to other relationships. There is no strictly negative suppression, and no purity of liberation from power.

'Apparatuses of security' were a form of governmentality that came after the development of discipline and did not displace discipline so much as superseded it and made it function to security's requirements. Security deals with the population as a whole, rather than isolating the sick to thoroughly diagnose and correct them each individually as in discipline. But security must rely on the proliferation of surveillance with its extensive diagnosis of pathologies for apparatuses to work on limiting any risks to the health and well-being of the species. And in putting discipline to work security shapes what gets watched, why, and from what perspective.

On January 18th 1978, (2008a, p.44-49), Foucault explained 'apparatuses of security' differed from discipline in four ways:

1. Discipline encloses and isolates the individual, security operates by constantly incorporating

larger circuits from production, psychology, behavior, to "the ways of doing things by producers, buyers, consumers, importers, and exporters" outward to the world market. Intervention can be aimed at details of the material or social environment in a way that can indirectly influence the well-being of the species as a whole.

2. Discipline tries to eliminate infractions down to the smallest detail, while security lets things happen. For example, the scarcity of food is not to be seen as evil but natural, and working within a reality of fluctuations. It is to be limited and canceled out without being prevented or eliminated. Scarcity will result in a rise in prices while a rise in prices will end scarcity by encouraging production. A process that results from scarcity will also stop it if allowed to

follow its course. Some people might starve because they cannot afford the food, but by letting some people die scarcity at the level of the population or species will not arise.

3. Discipline operates within deontic laws prescribing what is to be considered obligatory and forbidden; and what is not obligatory is forbidden. While security stands back to sufficiently grasp the point at which things are actually happening, whether or not they are desirable. The intent is to use a process's effective reality as a support to help make it function, or enable its components to function in relation to each other. While trying to respond to a particular part of reality in a way that aims to limit or negate that reality. "Regulation within the element of reality is

fundamental in apparatuses of security."
(Foucault 2004, p.46)

4. Discipline uses the imagination to imagine what should not happen, security uses reality for an analysis of not only what does happen but at the same time for what should happen. By allowing things to run their course, freedom in liberalism is not an idealistic part of ideology but a real part of a technology of power. The political technique of liberalism involves the interplay of reality with itself; allowing the free movement of men and things such that reality "follows its own course according to the laws, principles, and mechanisms of reality itself" (Foucault 2004, p.48) in a way that the dangers of this circulation are canceled out. Security relies on details that are neither good nor evil but necessary and inevitable natural processes

that, while not important in themselves, will

order something that is important because it

operates at the level of the population. The

wealth, resources and size of the population is

affected by the flows of currency, where it goes

or doesn't, as well as by the remote

international flows of imports and exports. By

tweaking details that seem far removed from

the overall level of the population in general,

(but which through statistical calculation,

analysis and reflection can be seen to actually

have an effect on it,) we can determine the

course and quality of the population.

The following week on January 25 1978 (2008a)
Foucault said that within reality there were constants and
regularities within the accidents that cannot be accurately
predicted. There is a single mainspring of action, desire,
that can promote the common good through modifying a

number of variables on which it depends. In liberal society the question becomes not of saying no to this but of encouraging responsible self-esteem with its beneficial effects. Government has to deploy procedures reflected within human nature and, with the help of it and in regard to it, aim at an objective it already has. Not only can we influence the course of a population through details that may seem remote, but the species is also the 'public' and this entails opinions, ways of doing things, forms of behaviour, customs, fears, prejudices, and requirements that can be influenced through education, campaigns and convictions.

On April 4 1979 (2008b) Foucault called civil society a discursive construction formed at the interplay of government with that which eludes it; the self-limitation of liberalism in dealing with economic processes. Foucault followed Adam Ferguson (1723-1816) in saying civil society contains the seeds of both politics and economics without being fully either. It is a pre-history that contains the bonds of hierarchical political solidarity, with some leading and others following, while also having the egoism of economic self-interests that divide society. Both trends give the community the dynamic historical development it has. For Foucault civil society was the independent environmental milieu to be affected/regulated by our policy interventions for the sake of the health and functioning of the species.

Lois McNay (2013) explained that discipline and freedom are not opposites that negate each other but are intertwined. Capitalism calls for active self-regulation rather than passive submission. Autonomy is not an obstacle, but one of its central technologies. Workers are no longer compelled to participate in capitalist production, but as entrepreneurs they are expected to bring to work an enthusiasm that treats it as a calling, going beyond the call of duty. Workers are to be given a voice and input into the policies of their enterprise; this will cut down on absenteeism and industrial accidents, but they are therefore also responsible for the success and failure of their company. The emancipatory element of personal freedom is eroded, and people assume responsibility for states of affairs they do not really control. Being an entrepreneur of ourselves means we should be willing to take on more risk; there is a compulsion to take on responsibility. Traditional theory assumes people naturally will their emancipation and this puts an absolute limit to power. But if autonomy is not a limit to social control but one of its central supports, how can we form effective opposition. Seeing others as competitors undermines solidarity with a resulting increase in depression and mental illness, emptying life of any meaning other than the profit motive. It atomizes society, reducing the state's responsibility to citizens, and erodes the collective values of duty and care.

Philip Mirowski (2013) criticizes the idea of being entrepreneurs of ourselves as the idea that nothing should stand in the way of success, certainly not one's old self, and nothing about the self is indispensable. (Charles Taylor called it the 'punctual self,' referring to John Locke.) We should cannibalize all parts of our self. We must be ready to try one role or persona after another, without any deeper commitment. Mirowski said that to portray the virtue of the market as giving people what they want is a bit disingenuous when people are portrayed as desperate to transform themselves into someone that wants what the market offers. The unreserved embrace of risk is supposed to be the primary method of changing one's identity to live life to the fullest. Since it is our choice it is perfectly justified, and any downside is something we brought upon ourselves. Mirowski's critique of Foucault is worth quoting at length. Foucault was wrong to assume the economy placed a limit to government intervention.

This is the exoteric truth; the esoteric truth is something else entirely.

> What Foucault missed were the critical notions of double truths... The neoliberals preach that the market is the unforgiving arbiter of all political action; *but they absolve themselves from its rule*. They propound libertarian freedoms but practice the most regimented hierarchy in their political organization; they sermonize about spontaneous order, while plotting to take over the state; they catechize prostration of the self before the awesome power of the knowledge conveyed by the market, but issue themselves sweeping dispensations. ... Their vision of governmentality elevates the market as a site of truth *for everyone but themselves*. If Foucault had taken this to heart, he would have had to revise his portrait of how regimes of truth validate power. (Mirowski, 2013, pp. 98-99)

In reality, the Mont Pelerin Society sees the free market as the ultimate site of truth for everyone but themselves. Hayek was inspired by his colleague at the University of Chicago, Leo Straus, with his double standard

214

of truth, esoteric secrets among the wise few and exoteric doctrines for the many masses. Neoliberalism seems to be at first sight a levelling doctrine that disparages elites and affirms the wisdom of crowds. But spontaneous order applies to everyone but themselves; they quite intentionally intervene when it is to their interests, like creating the Mont Pelerin Society with its international network of think tanks. They were already waiting with policy advice for when the Keynesian hegemony toppled. They went against the prevailing market and succeeded. Unfortunately, a double standard is corrupt and will rot our institutions from within. People may say they believe in the right standards/ideals and act accordingly, but those who "know" better will see it all as just political posturing for social control.

II. Social Insurance:
A Case for Collective Provision

Benoit Mandelbrot:
Markets are a lot Riskier than Theory allows,
as shown in the 2008 Crash.

Efficient Markets Hypotheses

According to John Quiggin (2010) the Efficient Market Hypothesis (EMH) said a stock price is the best estimate of the risk-adjusted value of future dividends and resale values. Financial markets make the best possible use of information, and the market is the most superior information processor of all relevant sources of risk. Financial markets are the best guide to the value of assets for investment and production decisions. The price at any given moment must be the 'right' one.

In its weak form the theory is no one can profit from predictions based on price history, price changes are independent. In its semi-strong form, the claim covers all public information, and in its strong form includes all information private or public. No insider trading. Profit is only possible where the EMF is not working or veers from the Black-Scholes estimated price. This means the market is just close enough to perfect that returns from exploiting any inefficiency is equal to the cost of skill and effort that goes into finding it. Therefore, it is only right the financial sector grow to take advantage of the more sophisticated economy. The upshot was the income and wealth of this sector grew phenomenally. Both American parties have been beholden to large donations from Wall Street. The financial sector seems to guarantee economic stability and prosperity. Unfortunately, the sector is more interested in discovering new forms of debt than new financial instruments for social security.

If stocks are the best summary of all relevant information, managers should only pay attention to short-term stock prices rather than long term interests because current share price is the best indicator of long-term share price. With the separation of owners and managers, many CEOs have run their company into the ground by only caring about the value of the stock options of the CEO. The higher the stock the more the short-term profit, even though long term casualties will not be known for some time. (Buckley, 2011, p. 56)

Theory says there is no need to worry about imbalances in savings and consumption, because income flows only reveal the present, while asset values contain all relevant information and an increase in them will reveal an increase in future income and consumption. On the contrary, Quiggin (2010) argues imbalances are the effect of financial market failures and the best means to correct it is to intervene by restricting unsound lending practices that drive such imbalances. But then the theory holds there are no market bubbles. If a bubble is seen speculators will sell their shares and if it continues short-sellers will come in selling shares they do not have to buy them back at a lower price. This way prices will return to their true value making speculators and short-sellers rich, so long as the bubble does not last longer than one's financial resources. Unfortunately, there is no way to tell how long a bubble will last. Since the only way to restrain the speculation driving such bubbles is to raise interest rates, it was thought the best thing to do was issue warnings. Though bubbles might lead to massively wasteful investment, it is said they also lead to innovations that are beneficial in the long-run. Supposedly in a well-developed modern market supervised by auditors and rating companies, irrational bubbles cannot be maintained. Then came the 2008 crash.

A History of the Ideologies of the Welfare State

Mandelbrot

Benoit Mandelbrot (2004) actually looked at a price series and found there were too many outliers and fat tails to be compatible with the normal distribution of a bell curve. In the short-term prices don't flow or glide, they jump all over the place. It doesn't settle down to an equilibrium, like a spinning top that will not slow down and reduce its fluctuations. In the graph below comparing the bell curve to the curve of a price series, the fat tails at the end reveal the extreme short-term stochastic values. Traditional theory assumes probabilities are evenly distributed like the bell curve of a coin toss. In markets, with a Cauchy or flat distribution, errors do not converge to a mean.

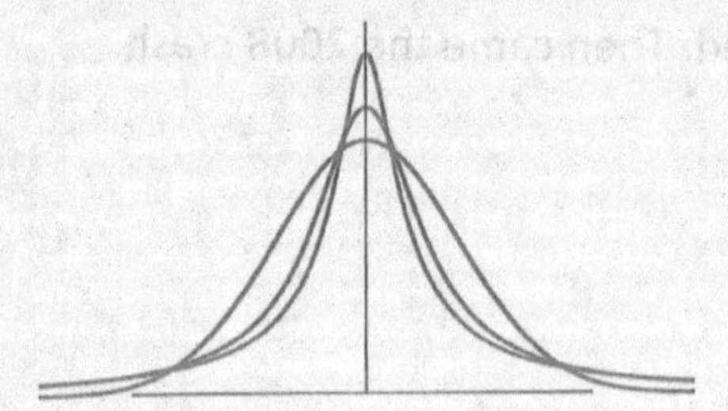

Comparing the Cauchy or Flat and the Gaussian or Bell-shaped

distributions (Mandelbrot, 2004, p. 40)

He also found long term dependencies; if a price goes up it will tend to go up, if it goes down it will tend to go down. He called these two characteristics the 'Noah' and 'Joseph' effects. A price series, thirdly, has unusual time variations not covered in theory, such that nothing will happen for extended periods and then everything happens at once, like in a baseball game. Time speeds up and slows down. The bell curve, or Gaussian distribution, was created to eliminate the noise of marginal errors found while studying the stable movements of planets. A market is much more turbulent. If the Dow Jones industrial average moves according to normal distribution, it will have moved 4.5% on only 6 days between 1996 and 2003. It moved that amount 366 times in that period. Rare events happen. According to Mandelbrot, markets are inherently uncertain, misleading, and bubbles are inevitable.

Portfolio Theory

Understanding this has important implications for finance theory. Modern portfolio theory has it that price fluctuations are independent. Just because one price goes down does not mean others will. One can compensate for differences in fluctuations if one spreads risk over a diversified portfolio with a lot of different stocks. Mixing riskier ones with safer ones is supposed to reduce one's overall risk. Winners offset losers. The prospect of profit was described by using only two numbers, reward and risk, or mean and variance. Risk is just how much price jumped around the mean. In the bell curve 'volatility' is variance and standard deviation, the latter is merely the square root of the former. The higher the variability of return, the riskier the asset. In comparing one stock to others one will be using covariance, so three numbers are used in portfolio calculations.

Then there is 'risk-aversion' to be considered. An efficient portfolio will produce the most profit with the least risk. Stocks can be rated with those of the most risk and greater return at the top for adventurists, and those with the least risk and lowest return at the bottom for the timid. The math is simplified when it is understood that all actors in a market will not have their own different portfolios, but only one for all. If one stock suggests an opportunity everyone will move in. Thus is born the 'stock-index fund,' a big pool of money from thousands of investors holding shares in the same proportion as the market overall. The value of a stock will depend only on its comparison with the rest of the market. Stocks must yield higher than the safer government bonds or T-bills. The difference is the 'equity risk premium.' The simplified math is called the Capital Asset Pricing model (CAPM), or to make the point that asset prices are ultimately determined by the preferences of consumers, it is also called the Consumption-based Capital Asset Pricing Model (CCAPM).

Collateral Debt Obligations (CDOs) applied portfolio theory to debt. All diverse kinds of debt are pooled into a portfolio with different tranches. The top tranche is a senior one that pays the lowest but investors collect their return first. The bottom tranche pays the highest but is the first to be wiped out. CDO^2, or synthetic CDOs, would take what was left over from previous CDOs and put them together into a CDO of CDOs then cut them up into tranches. When the 2008 crash hit because of improper underwriting standards in the mortgage market, all debts had been mixed up so no one knew where the toxic assets were, and derivatives were then considered worthless.

In opposition to EMH theory, with an interconnected economy a default in one area could lead to defaults in other areas. A massive crash first hit the mortgage market, then spread to all the CDOs which hit

224

the financial sector like a tsunami, then a depression hit the US economy as a whole, finally spreading around the world. No one thought a bubble bursting in mortgages would spread to economies everywhere, but it did. Paul Samuelson had argued financial markets were micro-efficient but macro-inefficient. The EMH worked better for individual stocks than for the aggregate. When a recession hit the whole economy would go down, not just an individual stock. When that happens the advice is to hold all shares until the economy bounces back, whenever it does, which creates the credit crunch.

Value at Risk

Pablo Triana (2009) explains that Value at Risk (VaR) estimates a bank's liabilities and exposure to losses by using a single number overall. It assumes 'rational expectations' where the future is expected to be like the past - which is generally true, until it isn't. Rare events are underestimated as extremely improbable. Volatility is based on past variance. Changes in a portfolio are assumed to be random and its frequency distribution can be estimated by a bell curve. This affects a bank's leverage and desire for liquidity.

Depending on the evaluation of risk, a bank may use more or less leverage with a given amount of equity. This will be the bank's 'capital adequacy requirement', the percentage of capital to risk-weighted assets. Because of deregulation there is no longer a mandatory liquidity ratio. Regulators hold that banks set their own rates according to VaR computer programs. Many US banks before the crash were leveraged at 30 or even 44 to one. Lehman Brothers was 97% debt to 3% equity. A mere drop of 3% would wipe out all shareholder's equity. (Buckley, 2011, pp. 39-40) Bear Stearns had USD 525 billion in assets and only USD 12 billion in equity, a leverage ratio of 44 times. Bear Stearns and Lehman brothers went bankrupt when the mortgage-backed CDOs defaulted, setting off the crash and the resulting credit crunch that hit other overstretched banks.

By underestimating the probability of rare events, banks, with little thought or worry, stretched themselves too thin, so that when the rain fell they got very wet, with enormous losses. VaR increased the damage. Extremely rare events happen in financial markets because of extreme turbulence. Because everyone adopted VaR the resulting landslide was worse. Dumping toxic assets to lower VaR increased the VaR. Risk may be evaluated when we know where the indeterminacy lies, but when we don't know what it is that we don't know the uncertainty is incalculable. People have tried to justify VaR as being better than nothing, but it can do immeasurable damage. The future is not exactly like the past and market variance is not normal. The market is a lot riskier than theory says it is.

The Need for Social Insurance, or What's Wrong with Foucault's Neoliberalism?

A clear economic case can be made for governments helping with risk, especially in compensating for imperfect information. Nicholas Barr (2001) has argued markets work better when:

a) consumer information is better,

b) goods are more cheaply and effectively improved,

c) the easier it is for consumers to understand available information,

d) the lower the cost of choosing badly, and

e) the more diverse the consumer's tastes.

Arguments for the public provision of medical care and education can be made accordingly. With medical care - information is often poor, people require individualized information which is not cheap, the information is highly technical, and the costs of mistakes can lead to death.

With education - parents may not be well informed,

228

improving information may not be cost effective, the emotional costs and the costs to a child's education from a wrong decision can be immense.

Barr goes on to explain social insurance is needed because private insurance can only provide for the individual, not everyone as in a natural disaster. Private insurance won't cover pre-existing conditions, and tries to use actuarial categories to assign risk. If risk is uncertain and unknown, no premium can be calculated. People can hide they are a bad risk, and moral hazard cannot be monitored enough. With social insurance membership is compulsory, preventing exit by those of minimal risk. This breaks the link between premium and individual risk. Barr argues social insurance can cope not only with risk itself but with uncertainty as well, such as when risk changes over time.

Going back in Canadian history, we can see a desire to pool resources together to fund social insurance by the end of the second world war. Leonard Marsh's *Report on Social Security for Canada* (1943) explained that, after the war, organized provisions for the 'risks and contingencies' of family life were to be prepared for those emergencies that were "beyond the capacity of most ... to finance adequately from their own resources." (Marsh, 1943, p. 7) He went on to say that in modern economic life "there are certain hazards and contingencies, which have to be met." (Marsh, 1943, p. 9) Some are completely unpredictable; others can be anticipated but not when. "They may be met in hit-and-miss fashion by individual families or they may be met by collective provision." (Marsh, 1943, pp. 9-10) Such problems are always being faced somewhere in the community or population. Quoting Rowell-Sirois, he wrote:

> It is impossible to establish a wage which will allow every worker to meet the heavy disabilities of serious illness, prolonged unemployment, accident and premature death. These are budget-shattering

contingencies that strike most unevenly. (Marsh, 1943, p. 10)

He said collective provision will make insurance against such dire circumstances more affordable. Many may be liable to a certain risk, but not everyone all the time. When disaster strikes, one can draw on the resources gathered from the contributions of many, including their own. There does not have to be a precise actuarial adjustment of premiums for the risk of each individual. Those who do not draw from the fund contribute to those who are the unlucky ones that are suffering. Social security can rely on taxes as well as contributions. This way state subsidies can be payable "without introducing the flavour of charity or the equal disability of irresponsible gratuity." (Marsh, 1943, p. 13) He argued for Unemployment and Health Insurance, Workmen's Compensation, Family Allowances, pensions, etc. Collective provisions are to fund the government's social insurance needed to cover everyone's risks. This may be considered socialist today but at the time it was bipartisan having the support of all Parties.

Moving forward, we see a concern with risk is central to Foucault's neoliberalism. As he explained on January 24th 1979, as a part of utilizing freedom a liberal society has had to accept certain risks and dangers. Government is therefore called upon to provide a social safety net.

> Roosevelt's welfare policy, ... starting from 1932, was a way of guaranteeing and producing more freedom in a dangerous situation of unemployment: freedom to work, freedom of consumption, political freedom, and so on. (Foucault, 2008b, p. 68)

Especially free markets; Keynes was supposed to save capitalism from itself. A Keynesian economic intervention, intended to guarantee both freedom and security from its dangers, is thought by neoliberals to actually undermine and curtail freedom. It is seen as counterproductive and is a crisis for liberalism, calling for new paths. Foucault said he did not share the neoliberal's paranoia about the complete monopolization and coercion of the state. They seem to have a desire to claw back the welfare state, even while they recognize the need for freedom with its inevitable risks. According to *The Oxford Handbook of the Welfare State* (Castles, Francis G., Leibfried, Stephen, Lewis Jane, Obinger, Herbert and Pierson, Christopher, 2010) the policies of the welfare state today include:

Old-Age Pensions

Health

Long-Term Care

Work Accident and Sickness Benefits

Disability

Unemployment Insurance

Labour Market Activation

Social Assistance

Family Benefits and Services

Housing

Education

A History of the Ideologies of the Welfare State

These are the risks and transitions one lives with in modern society. Since markets are so risky, there is a call for protection from risk even while promoting the neoliberal agenda of 'healthy' risk-taking.

There is a general agreement as to the need for some form of collective insurance. However, as Gøsta Esping-Anderson explained in *The Three Worlds of Welfare Capitalism* (1990) there has long been a serious debate over the distribution of benefits. The social democratic approach prefers universal social programs, while the liberal approach favours means-testing. Conservative countries existing from before the Enlightenment like Austria, Germany, France, and Italy may prefer to deliver their benefits according to one's status in a feudal type of corporatism, guilds turned into mutual societies. This was never a live option for Canada.

In pooling resources for universal programs, everyone pays into it so everyone should be able to benefit from it when needed. Something like socialized medicine or Medicare is universal because everyone and anyone gets sick at some point. Being human, we're all fallible and mortal. We're all in this together. Medicare is valued by many Canadians because it is shared. It is part of the national identity and one of the benefits of being a citizen. This democratic socialism can be contrasted to the liberal approach that prefers means-testing or giving to only the most-needy.

On March 7, 1979 (2008b, p.204-207) Foucault explained the French fascination with the negative tax as a welfare measure, was that it is means-tested. Assistance is not to be universal and given to everyone, to the benefit of the rich who contribute little. After having given up on full employment, the neoliberals don't care whether someone wants to work or not, the distinction between the deserving and undeserving poor is dropped. Assistance is targeted to the poor simply as a percentage/risk of the population; those whose income is below an absolute threshold, relative to each society.[1] Without however undermining the recipient's motivation to rise above that threshold; the exceptions being the very old and the disabled. All this makes sure no one is excluded from the economic game of consumption, while having a workforce in reserve when needed.

The choice between universal programs and means-testing is still a live issue that divides the left from the right among the Canadian electorate. Both approaches would destigmatize receiving benefits, except with means-testing you still must prove your poor enough or you don't get any help. Anyway, the 'social investment state' of Giddens' leftish neoliberalism focuses more on helping those ordinary citizens going through temporary

---

[1] This absolute threshold was intentionally devised to contrast with the socialist aim of moving towards an equality of incomes.

236

life transitions, than dealing with chronic impediments and larger social issues. With a slight shift of emphasis, we can either say the left was coopted by neoliberalism, which is a betrayal of left-wing values, or we can say there is a leftish version putting a friendly face on the neoliberal paradigm. Either way, the call is for citizens to take on more responsibility and govern themselves. We need citizens to work, but how we accomplish this can be empowering or punitive. We can see everyone as wanting to promote their self-esteem by working. Or, it can be that work has to be enforced as part of the social contract to alleviate resentment against the underserving poor. A person on welfare may have to take a job or at least look for one to obtain benefits. This has been called 'workfare.' At best the state can invest in training welfare dependants with new marketable skills, at worst it means accepting a dead-end menial occupation that doesn't really improve one's condition. The poor are thereby actively engaged in facilitating their own exploitation. Is self-responsibility a means of dumping burdens on the individual or a means of helping them help themselves?

We need to be free to help ourselves; our freedom is both at stake and at issue. According to Foucault, Liberalism consumes freedom and must produce a lot of it to function. Policy no longer depends on the wisdom of the sovereign but on the rationality of the governed. Freedom is not just part of an ideology but a real part of a technology of power. Foucault defined 'power' as conducting another's conduct. This contrasts with a situation where people have no choice but to do as they are told. 'Power' is where the free choices of individuals are affected by what governors may do, when they have a choice to obey or not. The negative income tax is designed to benefit the working poor, while workfare recipients must either "responsibly" look for work or risk being homeless with no support. We are forced to choose, to get busy with our life (consume and compete) if we are to take care of our needs. We are supposed to freely select our part-time, temporary, and self-employments as we would be filling out a resume; responsibly treating the jobs we are lucky enough to get as our higher calling. We are to be entrepreneurs of ourselves. How is it possible to liberate ourselves from manipulation and exploitation when it is our very freedom that is the means of social control?

Summary

Neoliberalism was not able to eliminate the welfare state, but there are two approaches to justifying it. The social investment state offers venture capital for citizens to invest in themselves and take on risk. Social insurance pools resources to help protect each other against risk. Gary Becker was a true neoliberal; a member of the Mont Pelerin Society and employed by the economics department at the University of Chicago. He pioneered 'economic imperialism' which supplies an economic analysis of non-economic phenomena. With the concept of 'human capital' he applies economics to our skills and education. Education is an investment in ourselves for future higher income. Friedman argued that since students are the ones benefitting from education they should be the ones bearing the cost, not the taxpayer. However, there are positive externalities from education, that outweigh the distortion of higher taxes. Such as having a critically sophisticated citizenry to discuss civic matters.

Anthony Giddens further developed onto Becker's idea of human capital the idea of the 'social investment state.' People should be encouraged to take more healthy risks and become less dependent on the welfare state. The state should supply money to the individual to invest in themselves during major periods of transition, like giving them their pensions early. People would rather see

240

themselves and others going to school than collecting the dole. Health and childcare are also important investments toward a productive workforce. The physical capital of infrastructure and the human capital of health and education all have positive externalities. Giddens was giving a friendly face to this neoliberal thinking by calling it a new form of social democracy.

For Giddens civil society could help unload some of the state's burdens bringing their governance closer to home, however it still needs to be independent from government in order to police it. For Robert Putnam civil society should build such social capital as trust, contacts, and mutual self-help in order to support tolerance, cooperation and respect, but not hatred and bigotry. How do we ensure this while respecting freedom of association, or free speech? The skills needed to operate civil organizations take time to learn; one cannot just throw money at the problem. Unfortunately, not everyone has the time, energy, nor inclination.

This has implications for the self, which is both a product of and tool for power. Foucault showed that in 'discipline' subjects are scientifically individuated through being compared to an average; a rank that can be raised or lowered, rewarded or penalized. This, it turns out, is a horror story. In prisons, the prisoner internalizes the paranoia of being caught without knowing it by those who watch them but whom they cannot watch. Punishment is a file that is never closed and can be used at any time to intervene in a subject's life, forcing them to spy on other delinquents. Recidivism, the fact those in prison tend to go back there, is the efficient result of this pyramid of surveillance.

Foucault said Gary Becker went one step better in arguing we do not have to psychoanalyze criminals, just punish them enough through fines and incarcerations. We do not have to go into any great depth, but merely change the economic environment to get the desired behaviour. Make the fines and penalties too expensive to ignore, don't analyze and control the subject down to the smallest detail. The question becomes not of saying no to our desires, but of encouraging responsible self-esteem with its beneficial effects. Government needs to deploy procedures reflected within human nature and, with the help of it and in regard to it, aim at an objective it already has while diminishing its dangers. But we are also supposed to introduce markets where they weren't before, so we can further our entrepreneurship of ourselves; to be someone who takes a chance to earn a profit and accepts the risk of a loss. Risk cannot be eliminated so it must be incorporated. It's even thrilling! We should be willing to cannibalize ourselves to want what the market offers, trying one role or persona after another without any deeper commitment in accord with the increase in part-time, temporary, and self-employment. We should strategically choose our next job as we would be filling out a resume portfolio. Taking such risks, the entrepreneur has become a modern-day popular hero.

Unfortunately, since the early 2000s a change has been imposed such that the responsibility for assuming risk has shifted from employers onto employees. Individuals have had to supply their own pensions, unemployment, and sickness benefits. But markets are a lot riskier than theory allows. The Efficient Markets Hypothesis, Portfolio Theory, and Value at Risk assume a normal bell curve distribution of independent variation, when markets are a lot more turbulent having extreme outcomes against tremendous odds. This is a reason to pool together to protect against events that can cripple one's resources, such as the 2008 crash. This was the point of social insurance. Maybe people should assume more responsibility for taking chances, but we still need a social safety net for when things fail. Is self-government and placing responsibilities on the individual a matter of empowering them or cynically dumping the burdens and concerns of the state on their shoulders? Is 'workfare' a means to improve our marketable skills or is it just another dead-end job? Is there a unique form of left-wing neoliberalism or has neoliberalism merely assimilated the left?

Bibliography

Althusser, L. (1971). Ideology and Ideological State Apparatuses. In L. Althusser, *On Ideology* (pp. 1-60). N.Y., N.Y.: Verso.

Baier, A. (1994). *Moral Prejudices: Essays on Ethics.* Cambridge: Harvard UP.

Barr, N. (2001). *The Welfare State as Piggy Bank: Information, Risk, Uncertainty, and the Role of the State.* N.Y., N.Y.: Oxford UP.

Beck, U. (1992). *Risk Society: Towards a New Modernity.* London: Sage Pub.

Becker, G. (1964). *Human Capital: A Theoretical and Empirical Analysis with Special Reference to Education.* Cicago: University of Cicago Press.

Berger, C. (1956). *The Writing on Canadian History: Aspects of English-Canadian Writing since 1900.* Toronto, Ont.: University of Toronto Press.

Bernstein, E. (1899/1993). *The Preconditions of Socialism.* N.Y., N.Y.: Cambridge UP.

Bosanquet, B. (1890). *The Philosophical Theory of the State.* London: Macmillon and Co.

Bradley, F. H. (1876). *Ethical Studies.* Oxford: Clarendon Press.

Bradshaw, Johnathan and Finch, Naomi. (2010). Family Benefits and Services. In F. G. Castles, S. Leibfried, J. Lewis, H. Obinger, C. Pierson, & S. L. Francis G. Castles (Ed.), *The Oxford Handbook of The Welfare State* (pp. 462-478). N.Y.: Oxford UP.

Brooks, Stephen and Menard, Marc. (2013). *Canadian Democracy: A Concise Introduction.* Don Mills: Oxford UP.

Buckley, A. (2011). *Financial Crisis: Causes, Context and Consequences.* Essex: Pearson Education Ltd.

Castles, Francis G., Leibfried, Stephen, Lewis Jane, Obinger, Herbert and Pierson, Christopher. (2010). *The Oxford Handbook of The Welfare State.* N. Y., N.Y.: Oxford UP.

Chambers, Simone and Kopstein, Jeffrey. (2006). Civil Society and the State. In J. S. Dryzeck, B. Honig, A. Philips, & B. H. JohnS. Dryzek (Ed.), *The Oxford Handbook of Political Theory* (pp. 363-381). N.Y., N.Y.: Oxford UP.

Cockett, R. (1994). *Thinking the Unthinkable: Think-Tanks and the Economic Counter-Revolution, 1931-1983.* London: Harper-Collins Pub.

Collins, R. (1998). *The Sociology of Philosophies: A Global Theory of Intellectual change.* Cambridge: Harvard UP.

Crosland, C. A. (1956). *The Future of Socialism*. Westport: Greenwood Press.

Dray, W. H. (1993). *Philosophy of History*. N.J.: Prentice-Hall Inc.

Emberley, P. (1996). *Zero Tolerance: Hot Button Politics in Canada's Universities*. Toronto: Penguin.

Esping-Anderson, G. (1990). *The Three Worlds of Welfare Capitalism*. Princeton: Princeton UP.

Fichte, J. G. (1794). *The Science of Knowledge.* (A. E. Kroegar, Trans.) London: Trubner and Co.

Foucault, M. (1975). *Discipline and Punish*. NY: Vintage Books.

Foucault, M. (1976). *The History of Sexuality Volume 1: An Introduction*. NY: Vintage Books.

Foucault, M. (1977/1984). Truth and Power. In M. Foucault, *The Foucault Reader* (pp. 51-75). NY: Vintage Books.

Foucault, M. (2008a). *Security, Territory, Population.* NY: Picador.

Foucault, M. (2008b). *The Birth of Biopolitics: Lectures at the College de France 1978-1979.* NY: Picador.

Francis, R. D. (1986). *Frank Underhill: Intellectual Provocateur.* Toronto: University of Toronto Press.

Friedman, M. (1962). *Capitalism and Freedom.* Chicago: University of Chicago Press.

Friedman, M. (1963). *The Great Contraction 1929-1933.* Princeton: Princeton UP.

Friedman, Milton and Schwartz, Anna Jacobson. (1963). *A Monetary History of the United States.* NJ: Princeton UP.

Giddens, A. (1998). *The Third Way: The Renewal of Social Democracy*. Malden, MA: Blackwell Pub.

Giddens, A. (2000). *The Third Way and its Critics*. Malden, MA: Polity Press.

Grant, G. (1965). *Lament for a Nation: The Defeat of Canadian Nationalism*. Toronto, Ont.: McGill-Queens.

Green, T. H. (1878-1882). *Prolegomena to Ethics*. Oxford: Clarendon Press.

Green, T. H. (1879-1880). *Lectures on the Principles of Political Obligation*. London: Longman, Green, and Co.

Gutstein, D. (2014). *Harperism: How Stephen Harper and His Think Tank Colleagues have Transformed Canada*. Toronto, Ont.: James Lorimer and Co.

Gutting, G. (2001). *French Philosophy in the Twentieth Century.* Cambridge: Cambridge UP.

Hacker, J. (2006). *The Great Risk Shift: The New Economic Insecurity and the Decline of the American Dream.* N.Y., N.Y.: Oxford UP.

Harcourt, B. (2011). *The Illusion of Free Markets: Punishment and the Myth of Natural Order.* Cambridge: Harvard UP.

Hayek, F. (1944). *The Road to Serfdom.* Chicago: University of Chicago Press.

Hayek, F. (1945). The Use of Knowledge in Society. *Library of Economics and Liberty.*

Hayek, F. (1949/1967). The Intellectuals and Socialism. In F. Hayek, *Studies in Philosophy, Politics, and Economics.* Chicago: University of Chicago Press.

Hayek, F. (1960). *The Constitution of Liberty.* Chicago: U of Chicago Press.

Hayek, F. (1967). Principles of a Liberal Social Order. In F. Hayek, *Studies in Philosophy, Politics, and Economics.* Chicago: University of Chicago Press.

Hegel, G. W. (1821/1991). *Elements of the Philosophy of Right.* (H. B. Nisbet, Trans.) Cambridge: Cambridge UP.

Heidegger, M. (1962). *Being and Time.* (J. M. Robinson, Trans.) N.Y., N.Y.: Harper Collins Pub.

Hobhouse, L. T. (1911). *Liberalism.* N.Y., N.Y.: Oxford UP.

Hobhouse, L. T. (1918). *The Metaphysical Theory of the State.* London: George Allen & Unwin, Ltd.

Hobson, J. A. (1909). *The Crisis of Liberalism: New Issues of Democracy.* Westminster: Orchard House.

Horowitz, G. (1966, May). Conservatism, Liberalism, and

>Socialism in Canada: An Interpretation. *Canadian*

>*Journal of Economics and Political Science, 32*(1),

>143-171.

Jenson, J. (2010). Continuities and Change in the Design of

>Canada's Social Architecture. In J. C. Smith, & J. C.

>Smith (Ed.), *The Oxford Handbook of Canadian*

>*Politics* (pp. 417-433). N.Y., N.Y.: Oxford UP.

Jones, D. S. (2012). *Masters of the Universe: Hayek,*

>*Friedman, and the Birth of Neoliberal Politics.* N.J.:

>Princeton UP.

Kant, I. (1781). *Critique of Pure Reason.* (N. K. Smith,

>Trans.) N.Y., N.Y.: Macmillan Co.

Kenworthy, L. (2010). Labour Market Activation. In S. L.

>Francis G Castles, *The Oxford Handbook of The*

>*Welfare State* (pp. 435-447). N.Y.: Oxford UP.

King, Desmond and Ross, Fiona. (2010). Critics and Beyond. In F. G. Castles, S. Leibfried, J. Lewis, H. Obinger, C. Pierson, & S. L. Francis G. Castles (Ed.), *The Oxford Handbook of The Welfare State* (pp. 45-57). N.Y., N.Y.: Oxford UP.

Kuhnle, Frank and Kaufmann, Franz-Xaver. (2010). The Emergence of the Welfare State. In F. G. Castles, S. Leibfried, J. Lewis, H. Obinger, C. Pierson, & S. L. Francis G. Castles (Ed.), *The Oxford Handbook of the Welfare State* (pp. 61-80). Oxford: Oxford UP.

Leacock, S. (1920). *The Unsolved Riddle of Social Justice*. London: John Lake and the Bodley Head Ltd.

League for Social Reconstruction. (1935). *Social Planning for Canada*. Toronto: Thomas Nelson and Sons.

Mandelbrot, B. (2004). *The (Mis)behaviour of Markets: A Fractal View of Financial Turbulence*. N.Y., N.Y.: Basic Books.

Marchildon, G. (2010). HealthCare. In J. C. Smith, J. C.

    Courtney, D. E. Smith, & J. C. Smith (Ed.), *The*

    Oxford Handbook of Canadian Politics (pp. 434-

    450). N.Y., N.Y.: Oxford UP.

Mares, I. (2010). Macroeconomic Outcomes. In F. G.

    Castles, S. Leibfried, J. Lewis, H. Obinger, C. Pierson,

    & S. L. Francis G. Castles (Ed.), *The Oxford*

    Handbook of The Welfar State (pp. 539-551). N.Y.,

    N.Y.: Oxford UP.

Marsh, L. (1943). *Report on Social Security for Canada*

    1943. Toronto: University of Toronto Press.

Marshall, T H and Bottomore, Tom. (1950). *Citizenship and*

    Social Class. London: Pluto Press.

McKillop, A. B. (1979). *A Disciplined Intelligence: Critical*

    Inquiry and Canadian Thought in the Victorian Era.

    Montreal: McGill-Queen's UP.

McKillop, A. B. (1994). *Matters of the Mind: The University in Ontario 1791-1951.* Toronto: University of Toronto Press.

McNay, L. (2013). Contemporary Critical Theory. In M. Freedan, L. T. Sargent, M. Stears, & L. T. Michael Freedan (Ed.), *The Oxford Handbook of Political Ideologies* (pp. 138-154). N.Y., N.Y.: Oxford UP.

McQuaig, L. (1991). *The Quick and the Dead: Brian Mulroney, Big Business and the Seduction of Canada.* Toronto: Viking.

McQuaig, L. (1995). *Shooting the Hippo: Death by Deficit and other Canadian Myths.* Toronto, Ont.: Penguin.

Mirowski, P. (2011). *Science-Mart: Privatizing American Science.* Cambridge: Harvard UP.

Mirowski, P. (2013). *Never Let a Serious Crisis Go to Waste: How Neoliberalism Survived the Financial Meltdown.* N.Y., N.Y.: Verso.

Mises, L. v. (1949). *Human Action: A Treatise on Economics*. Indianapolis: Liberty Fund, Inc.

Neil, R. (1991). *A History of Canadian Economic Thought*. London: Routledge.

Nozick, R. (1974). *Anarchy, State, and Utopia*. NY: Basic Books.

O'Neill, J. (1998). *The Market: Ethics, Knowledge, Politics*. London: Routledge.

Owram, D. (1986). *The Government Generation:Canadian Intellectuals and the State 1900-1945*. Toronto: University of Toronto Press.

Peikoff, L. (1991). *Objectivism: The Philosophy of Ayn Rand*. NY: Meridian.

Plehwe, Dieter and Walpen, Bernard. (2006). Between Network and Complex Organization: The Making of Neoliberal Knowledge and Hegemony. In D.

Plehwe, B. Walpen, & G. Neunhoffer, *Neoliberal Hegemony: A Global Critique* (pp. 27-50). London: Routledge.

Putnam, R. (2000). *Bowling Alone: The Collapse and Revival of American Community*. N.J.: Princeton UP.

Quiggin, J. (2010). *Zombie Economics: How Dead Ideas Still Walk Among Us*. N.J.: Princeton UP.

Rothbard, M. (1962). *Man, Economy, and State: A Treatise on Economic Principles*. Los Angeles: Nash Publishing Corporation.

Rothbard, M. (1963). *America's Great Depression*. NY: Stellar Editions.

Rothbard, M. (2002). *The Ethics of Liberty*. NY: NY UP.

Skelton, O. D. (1911). *Socialism: A Critical Analysis*. N.Y., N.Y.: Houghton Mifflin.

Triana, P. (2009). *Lecturing Birds on Flying: Can Mathematical Theories Destroy the Financial Markets?* N.J.: Wiley.

Wright, S. (2018). Virtue Responsibilism. In N. Snow, *The Oxford Handbook of Virtue* (pp. 747-764). Oxford: Oxford UP.

Liberal/Democracy 2003

The term 'liberal democracy' seems to imply a symbiotic combination of two sets of demands, one private and one public. I intend to show that the two ideologies are not always in harmony, and in fact, may even conflict with one another. Liberalism may be distinguished from democracy on four counts.

1. The former protects negative liberty, while the latter promotes positive liberty.
2. One concentrates on the individual, while the other stresses community.
3. One favours legal rights, while the other includes political negotiation.
4. Public decision-making in one is more procedural, while in the other it is more substantive.

So far, liberalism/capitalism has won over democracy. However, there is empirical evidence that within most

A History of the Ideologies of the Welfare State

developed liberal democracies, people are starting to question the status quo and are demanding more participation in the decisions that affect their lives.

Negative and Positive Liberty

Liberalism and democracy seem united in their call to freedom. There is a difference, however, in the kind of freedom each demand. In 'Two Concepts of Liberty,' Isaiah Berlin (1969) distinguished between two kinds of liberty. One he called negative and the other positive. Negative liberty was freedom from interference. "If I am prevented by others from doing what I could otherwise do, I am to that degree unfree. (p.122) Positive liberty was defined as being one's own master, not controlled or manipulated by outside forces. This sense of freedom is the ability to accomplish something positive rather than the absence of restraint. Aside from Berlin, the common use has been to

262

contrast negative and positive liberty as "freedom from ..."
and "freedom to ..."

Jean-Jacques Rousseau wrote that man could be forced to be free. For those who believe in negative liberty this would be nonsense and self-contradictory. In so far as one is being forced, one is to that extent not free. While Rousseau had a knack for turning an ironic phrase, he was in this case being sincere. He was saying we should be made to take control of our own lives. This would be the positive freedom to self-actualize. An example would be the kind of "tough love" where parents force a child out of the house at a certain age in order for them to become self-reliant. It is a measure taken to ensure the young adult becomes more mature; to force them out of their non-age or adolescence. Maturity would include the responsibility to regulate oneself according to law.

Laws are necessary. We need rules by which to coordinate the activities that take place in a modern society. To call for negative freedom is not asking to do whatever we please. Such things as stopping at a red light may deter us from going forward, but this would hardly be an infringement on our freedom because it is so trivial. Theft or assault are things that no society can permit. Liberals like John Stuart Mill have justified such limitations on one's options by saying that we should be free to do whatever we want as long as it does not harm anyone else or interfere with the ability of others to do what they want. A democracy would demand the positive liberty to set its own standards. Self-determination means that a polity should be able to enact its own laws, rather than being forced to do it by someone else. This is the self-mastery to draw up legislation. To secure negative freedom we need laws, and this entails the positive liberty to set those laws. Here liberalism and democracy compliment each other in their demand for freedom. This harmony is precarious, however, because the different demands may try to override each other.

Isaiah Berlin feared that with positive liberty the state would go too far in demanding conformity. John Stuart Mill called this the 'tyranny of the majority.' A liberal would fear that without the protection of a strong negative liberty, minorities might be discriminated against. For example, a Protestant state might force all its Catholic citizens to abandon their religion. The liberal has demanded a clear line be drawn between the private, where the state has no say, and the public, which is open to policy. If a state is not to devolve into a totalitarian regime there has to be constitutional limits placed upon its power. According to C. B. Macpherson (1976), the biggest fear the liberals had when opening up democracy to universal franchise was that since the poor were the greatest in number, there might be pressure for the government to produce class legislation. Capitalists wanted their property rights to be free from socialist policies. Property was declared private and corporations were given the legal status of individuals. In promoting negative liberty, liberals have always been concerned with protecting the private individual from the interference from the state. In serving positive liberty on the other hand, democracy has involved the decisions of groups and communities to forge their own agendas, living standards, and legislation.

Individualism and Communitarianism

Liberals and democrats hold contrasting psychological and sociological theories. The former takes as its model the 'economic man.' The individual's needs are taken as exogenous. They are a 'given' and not up to dispute. Desires are pure data. They are neither right nor wrong, true nor false. They just are. An agent is self-defined and knows what he wants before entering any

266

transaction. There is a pre-given reason why anyone would do anything. The economic man is a rational utility maximizer. People are seen as seeking the most pleasure possible, while avoiding as much pain as possibly. They want to get as much as they can for as little as they can. They aim to do little work for big rewards. This is called efficiency. Exerting effort is not the only disutility, however, there is also opportunity cost. To buy one thing a person has to forego another, given a limited budget. In order to participate in one activity, one has to give up doing something else at the same time. Given present wants, one needs to decide whether it is worth the trouble, or whether there is something else he'd rather have. Having made a decision, one can then choose to enter a transaction, aiming to get as much out of it as he can. This is instrumental reason. A relationship may have commitments but one has already consented to them by choosing to enter into it in the first place, and if he later

267

finds it is not worth the hassle he can opt for something better. Since one is self-sufficient before any social contact, he can see whether it is meeting his needs or choose other means that are more appropriate. An economic transaction would not occur unless both parties were likely to benefit. Each has what the other wants so we trade; if there's a better deal elsewhere we'd go there. With each seeking the most satisfaction, the better off everyone is, theoretically. This ideal scenario does not take into consideration the bonds people have with one another as members of a community.

Communitarians, on the other hand, people are what they are because of the social roles they play. People are defined by the interactions they live. Without a social context within which to orient themselves they would be lost and without identity. One can be a parent, friend, academic, or a citizen because these roles pre-exist as possibilities in society, defining who people are. One tries to give his best to the larger whole, which is what gives meaning to life. It is what makes one worthy of being valued by ourselves and others. This is not to say he would not have human dignity without these interactions, but that his existence is richer because of them. This is contrasted to utility maximization because the more one puts into activities the more one gets out of them. One would not be using people for his own ends, because he is fulfilling himself through caring for the needs of others. In democracy, he can become a participant of the group in making a decision, proud to benefit his neighbors. He can belong as a member, and be at home among his peers by exercising his freedom.

Referring back to the two concepts of freedom, it can be said that negative liberty allows for maximum outcome by letting each individual get what he can for the best deal he can. Positive liberty exercises the potential to contribute as part of a team in making a difference to how a person lives. In negative liberty the individual is free to buy the selections offered, while positive liberty may open new possibilities by putting alternative agendas on the table. The economic man takes the options given by those who manufacture products, but this is alright since they are catering to needs that are already there. A lobby group tries to ensure there are more avenues available than the status quo, or objects to projects that are demeaning. Thereby they have a say in what options are available, and can change what people think they need. Rather than accepting values as irrational data, they can be publicly articulated and debated – such things as social welfare, public goods, and constitutions. Thus it is important how people communicate with each other through public facilities, whether in courts or assemblies. One is based on the discourse of rights; the other is a path toward consensus.

Rights and Negotiations

There have been different ways in which rights have been justified. If we start with man as a rational maximizer then, like John Stuart Mill, we may try to use utilitarianism to determine rights. The state, for example, should not impose a preferred way of life because Mill believed general welfare would be better off in the long run. However, this justification leaves rights vulnerable. For example, Mill also thought we should give the educated more votes so the result would be more informed. If most people would be much happier at the expense of only a few, then rights could be in jeopardy.

Avoiding reliance on anything contingent and fallible, Immanuel Kant thought that our rights could be determined from conditions of rational thought. To avoid the fundamental error of contradiction, we must will our acts as if they were universal. We would need to ask ourselves "What if everyone did that?" This would mean that the rule of law applied to everyone equally. The second condition was that we don't use people but treat them as ends in themselves; capable of determining their own goals and values. This is described as the right of autonomy. Rights would be more secure as assumptions of fair play than as tools to increase our utility. Rights would have priority over any conception of the good life. To be just, the state must not impose what it thinks is good. It must not be biased. This is the precondition of the equality of rights which enables the possibility of an ethical society and discourse. Reason determines out of itself, by its own bootstraps, the idea of self-entailed freedom. Just as the choosing-self is prior to the inclinations it chooses, the right is prior to the good for all autonomous individual's. Without appealing to the way things are, however, Kant is left with a criterion that is vacuous. There is no way to decide what society should be like, other than harmonizing the wills of rational maximizers. With the contentless notion of autonomy – freedom from all external influences, desires, traditions, and authorities – we would renounce everything and end up in total destruction. Such rights, freedoms, and imperatives are purely formal, and people need a more concrete direction to guide and justify their actions.

In contrast to the individualism of Kant, Hegel would say people get the concept of a concrete ethics from the customs that are a part of the community within which they are situated. Since human beings are what they are because of the society in which they live and the social roles they perform, they are called upon to accept an obligation to the good of the community they inhabit. Social values define the individual, his rights and corresponding duties. 'Human Rights' which include education, a decent standard of living, and medical treatment, are an ideal conception of how life ought to be and favors the development of specific capacities. A life that fell short of these would be inhumane. In contradiction to Kantian thought, the good is prior to the right. One's rights are supported by the commonwealth of which one is a citizen. In turn, our duty is to support the world we enjoy. We need to negotiate a partnership where the goal of the individual is to contribute to the greater good, while the role of society is to empower its members. There needs to be give and take between valued and respected parties. One may have the right not to help out, but that would not make it right to do that. One may be called upon to compromise or even sacrifice, for things such as taxes and war. Morally the common good has some priority over rights. People need to live up to standards other than their own self-interest. Individuals partake in a social life, which is going on anyway, but people help to realize its value and make this actual through living their lives. It is when our institutions, which embody certain ethical world views, are no longer seen as justifiable, or have become travesties, that men become alienated and turn to themselves for their identity. That is when society would disintegrate and would have to reason out a new legitimate form of public rationality, so that people can identify with a new set of virtues. Hence, the importance of freely forming public opinion would be to develop a social life by which we could abide. The liberal could retort that "community" is a metaphysical entity which does not exist and such talk is merely propaganda. Community is just an abstraction made up of individuals with their inalienable natural rights.

The actual list of fundamental rights has been problematic and somewhat different for each constitution. Locke defined our rights as 'life, liberty, and property.' The American Declaration of Independence affirmed rights to 'life, liberty, and the pursuit of happiness.' The Canadian constitution of 1982 has declared that "everyone has the following fundamental freedoms:

a) Freedom of conscience and religion;

b) Freedom of thought, belief, opinion and expression, including freedom of the press and other media of communication;

c) Freedom of peaceful assembly; and

d) Freedom of association."

Constitutions essentially clarify the boundaries of the state, defining its role and separating it from the economy and civil society.

Besides declaring property as private and developing an economy separate from government, a healthy liberal democracy has also needed free public space in order to develop a strong civil society outside the tutelage of government. The negative logic of the liberal and the positive logic of the democrat, however, would disagree about the relationship society should play in regard to the state. The former would argue that the job of those outside the government would be to blow the

276

whistle when government was corrupt or when it overstepped its bounds, hence the scandalous news clips and the rising demand to recall public representatives. On the other hand, democrats would argue that a free society outside government control is necessary to form public opinion. The first is the role of the watchdog, the second is to facilitate discussion. The Fundamental Freedoms in the Canadian Constitution were made for ensuring open debate – to critique and improve the government, thereby making it more responsive to the people. The first agenda would keep guard over the just state, protecting the autonomy of individuals. The second agenda follows Hegel in trying to give direction to the state through the freedom of rational thought to determine the 'good life' in ongoing debate. The American system of rights protects the negative liberty of the individual from the threat of being killed, from governments stepping on freedoms, and from interference with the pursuit of happiness however that's

A History of the Ideologies of the Welfare State

understood. Canadian fundamental freedoms promote the positive liberty of freely forming public opinion.

In 'Liberal Politics and the Public Sphere' (1995, p.276) the Canadian Charles Taylor said that ...

> The conditions for a genuine democratic decision can't be defined in abstraction from self-understanding. They include
>
> a) That the people concerned understand theselves as belonging to a community that shares some common purposes and recognizes its members as sharing in these purposes;
> b) That the various groups, types, and classes of citizens have been given a genuine hearing and were able to have an impact on the debate; and
> c) That the decision emerging from this is really the majority preference."

Taylor wrote that in a society of mutually disinterested individuals all we could hop for was (c) and maybe (b).

278

With each individual into their own life plan, why would they listen to another's point of view? However, (b) would be greatly affected by (a). A sense of being heard depends upon a feeling of being valued and respected by other groups. Conciliation is destroyed by conflict. Taylor argues that rights enhance discord through emphasizing the importance of judicial review. In court there are clear winners and losers, where winners take all and there is no opportunity to compromise. In discourse to declare something a right is to end debate. The possibility of forming majority coalitions can disintegrate into a variety of narrow interests designed to mobilize litigation more effectively. Fragmentation can frustrate the formation of a common purpose and the power to carry that out, making it seem like a waste of time. Alienating people into individualism would, in turn, exacerbate the problem of undermining solidarity. This problem makes some tough issues harder to resolve. Areas where we need to come to a consensus, where there is some give and take and some sacrifice involved, are harder to achieve because of a lack of sympathy and fellowship. Cooperation may be imperative but not forthcoming, if people don't care enough to reconcile their differences.

To avoid fragmentation, some democratic writers of the past have believed there should only be one class or no classes. While this may not be possible, some countries have tried to curb the extremes of wealth and poverty through effective redistribution of income, thereby lessening the division between the well-off and the less fortunate. These measures toward equality could be a way of creating a more cohesive society, but can be seen as infringing on the rights of the wealthy.

In comparing this kind of equality with that of Kant's we may call the latter, formal equality before the law, and the former equality of condition and political power. As we have seen, liberal capitalists wanted their

280

private property protected from class legislation, and human rights have demanded a decent standard of living. In *Democracy and Capitalism* (1987) Samuel Bowles and Herbert Gintis have explained the clash between property rights and personal rights as the main contradiction of modern social thought. Yet, equality in the way we combine our interests is essential to the formation of public decisions.

Procedural and Substantive Decision Making

Following liberal logic, democracy is reduced to a formal procedure for making public choices among given alternatives. Voting gets input from each individual separately through a secret ballot and compiles them to see which option has the highest count. Rousseau called this the 'will of all' and contrasted it with the 'general will' which was the result of the combined effort of everyone to come to an agreement. Hegel called aggregative elections the result of a "heap," or shall we say a mass society. It would not be differentiated into clear rational articulation. Agreement does not have to mean that we are all the same, think the same, and that for purposes of collective debate we have to be treated the same. Our differences can be recognized and incorporated into a more complex understanding of the public good.

With a group of mutually disconnected individuals there can be a lack of support for public goods. A public good is one that benefits everyone. A lighthouse helps all ships, but is not able to charge each one for its services. Rational maximizers would then avoid paying wherever possible, shifting the burden for its preservation onto others. This is called the free rider problem. It is evident in low turnouts at elections. "Other people are making the decisions anyway so why should I bother?" It seems so little to ask one wonders why people avoid it? Being able

282

to vote every few years to see who will run the country allows for very little input and citizens need to see they are having an effect. Sustaining a true democracy demands civic virtue and this cannot be extracted from isolated uninvolved individuals. To get people more interested and participatory, governments have tried processes of integration to get people working together toward agreements.

Integrative processes involve coming to a consensus. There is give and take, but it demands a rather profound knowledge of the area under discussion. The possible resolutions are open-ended. This means career politicians must be authorities on the matter. The process tends to be elite driven and therefore limitedly accessible to the common man. However, it has been possible to send experts into communities for input and get agreement from the populace, such as the town meetings of the Charlottetown Accord. This involves decentralizing power so democracy functions from the grassroots up. The danger with this process is the possible fragmenting of local groups from the national level. In the end, aggregative and integrative processes are merely means to achieve decisions.

More is demanded from democracy than just coming to conclusions. Liberals try not to prejudge the good life; by following rules of the right method one will arrive at the correct answer. Kant thought that all we needed were the correct formal procedures involving the rule of law and equal rights. Hegel criticized this for not giving more content to the good life of the community. Democracy is more substantive because it is a way of life, preferable to other procedures because it brings people together. To have freely negotiated public opinion involves a concrete standard about the quality of life we share. It can even imbue the whole of society with justice by addressing the way we treat each other, outside the narrow focus of government. Power is not homogenized but comes in many forms, from the patriarchal father to the greedy employer. Anywhere that people can have input into the decisions that affect their lives is theoretically open to democratic influence, from the family to the workplace. People seem increasingly to demand more empowerment to effect change, and this requires that we listen to each other with respect and consideration. Democracy may even assume a standard by which to judge some of the conclusions we reach, since the content of the good life includes community, collaboration, and some political equality of condition. Thus, the difference between liberalism and democracy can be radical.

Conclusion

This paper has discussed many ideas about liberalism and democracy, but in one sense it is very simple. The contrast is between the protection of the autonomy of individual choice versus the empowerment of community decision. On the other hand, these two world views have very deep differences with vast implication. In practice we call ourselves a liberal democracy, but this has been more liberal than democratic. People have had their power truncated, allowing political and business elites to determine their lives for them. This is called representative democracy, however people's expectations have been changing. In 'The Decline of Deference' (1996), Neil Nevitte has used World Values Surveys which report results from more than forty countries, covering over seventy percent of the world's population. Concentrating on the most advanced nations of Europe and North America, he has been able to show interesting changes in people's attitudes. Over the last twenty years there has been a declining reliance on primary resources and manufacturing, and a rising increase in knowledge-based and technological services. We may call these countries post-industrial. For those born after the Second World War, scarcity has been less of an issue and people are more concerned with quality of life. Nevitte calls this post-materialism. People are becoming more assertive and less compliant. There has been decreasing confidence in governments and a corresponding rise in support for the free market. Old style socialism may be currently passé, but capitalism is not entirely secure either. An increasing willingness to pursue unconventional forms of political action such as signing petitions or joining boycotts have been strongly correlated with a demand for a stronger voice in workplace decisions. This is closer to participatory democracy. The finale result is impossible to determine, but it is suggestive of the desire for change.

A History of the Ideologies of the Welfare State

Bibliography

Berlin, Isaiah 1969: 'Two Concepts of Liberty' in *Four Essays on Liberty.* NY: Oxford UP.

Bowles, Samuel and Gintis, Herbert 1987: *Democracy and Capitalism.* Basic Books.

Macpherson, C.B. 1976: *The Life and Times of Liberal Democracy.* Oxford UP.

Nevitte, Neil 1996: *The Decline of Deference.* Peterborough: Broadview Press.

Sandel, Michael J. 1995: 'The Political Theory of the Procedural Republic' in *Political Ideologies and Political Philosophies.* Ed. H.B. Mc Collough, Toronto: Thomson Educational Publishing, inc.

Taylor, Charles 1979: *Hegel and Modern Society.* Cambridge UP

Taylor, Charles 1995: 'Liberal Politics and the Public Sphere' in *Philosophical Arguments.* Cambridge: Harvard UP.

288

Are Canadian MPs 'Trained Seals'? 11/14/14

Pierre Trudeau once said "when they are 50 yards from Parliament Hill, they are no longer honourable members, they are just nobodies." Even within the House Honourable Members may be nobodies. I will discuss four functions of Canadian MPs then turn to the suggested reforms for making the opposition, backbenchers and committees more powerful. In the end Canadian MPs should not be seen as merely trained seals, at least not without qualification.

The Functions of Canadian MPs

The Government of Canada webpage says the roles of MPs depend upon where they are, such as in the House of Commons during Question Period, Committees (Standing, Ad Hoc, or Joint etc.), Party Caucuses, and in their constituency or parliamentary offices. These roughly

A History of the Ideologies of the Welfare State

correspond to four functions for Canadian Members of Parliament: committees for writing laws and authorizing expenditures, surveillance of the government and administration in the House, constituency services in their offices and caucuses, with an overall educational function of shaping public discourse. The first two functions contradict each other as the legislature tries to pass bills expediently while also trying to critique each bill in turn (Franks 1971).

In first past the post elections for single member constituencies, the candidate with the most votes in their riding wins a seat. The leader of the party with the most seats in the House of Commons forms the executive who appoints the ministers of his cabinet from the elected members of his party. Almost all legislation is initiated in the Prime Minister's Office. If a party has a majority of seats 50%+1 legislation is bound to go through. Minority governments are relatively rare 13/41, because they rely

290

on concessions to stay in office they usually last less than two years. Bills go through three readings. The first usually has little debate and there is a momentum for them to be passed. Substantive amendments have to be introduced during second reading or risk being ruled out of order later. Since 1968 all legislation is considered in detail by standing committees, restricted to merely modest refinements of the details. These standing committees are made up according to the proportion of the parties' seats in the House, with Cabinet Members usually acting as chairpersons. The minister of a House majority does not have to accept suggested changes and can replace members that conflict with them. The third reading is followed by royal assent and proclamation by the Governor General.

Rather than forming independent legislation, opposition MPs focus on scrutinizing bills. The House of Commons Oral Question Period is the most effective means to embarrass the government, if they are not doing a good job. Since the introduction of TV cameras, people have complained about the negative theatrics and 'mindless adversarialism.' It is, however, the best way to publicize issues and affect the forms of debate. If the government loses a high priority legislation or the budget is disallowed the result can be that the government loses the confidence of the House and an election is called by the Governor General. Party discipline for a majority government usually means legislation goes through. However, the outcome of debate can be influenced by public opinion in a way that can be unpredictable. Question Period distorts and magnifies the public's image of parliament as full of conflict, when the truth is committees rely on conciliation and negotiation. "The adversarial nature of Canadian politics obscures the fact that these partisan disagreements take place within a fairly narrow band of consensus on basic values." (Brooks

292

and Menard 2013 p.258) While the opposition can publicize the faults of the government, the problem is they may have little direct impact on amending legislation. They may however form the next government at election.

Constituency service takes up most of an MP's time. This may personally involve an MP in contacting public service officials, or airing grievances in the House. Caucuses can be used by backbenchers to air the grievances of their region to their own party. Such work can involve an MP keeping in touch with their riding, or communicating government policy and gaining support through yearly newsletters and personal face-to-face contact. Constituency service could also involve a staff member directing a constituent to the right federal department. The ombudsman role may help the MP in their parliamentary role but it may not and can compete with it for time and attention without helping their re-election. MPs are given enough funds to hire support staff such as secretaries, two at the Ottawa office and two at the constituency office, but they are not given enough to hire policy analysts and research staff.

Parliament is a legitimizing institution that holds the government accountable. Actions of the government must be approved by the House. Representation can be seen as involving a proportional representation of seats in the House according to the mix of the general population: gender, ethnicity, class, age, etc. Though people may not trust their politicians they do tend to approve the parliamentary institutions. MPs are the *parler* in parliament and can draw attention to controversial parts of the government's performance. (Brooks and Menard 2013 p.260) Opposition can mobilize public opinion, especially if MPs could coordinate their efforts with interest groups and stakeholders for behind-the-scenes lobbying. However, only parliament has what Sheldon Wolin (1960/2004 p.384-389) called an 'integration function' where they are to represent the interests of the common good for the entirety of the whole diversity of their citizens/subjects. Special interests only represent their particular members. MPs are supposed to give priority to national interests over local ones. Committees actively seek public input and travel across the country to do so.

Possible Reforms

In 1973, before the creation of the Reform Party, J. A. A. Lovink discussed the merits of three parliamentary reforms. The first two were proposed in 1968. 1) Reform of the standing committee system would involve increasing their research funds, expanding their scope, and releasing them from party discipline. 2) Abolition of the 'confidence convention' which forces MPs to support measures they find dubious. There should be a distinction between first order legislation which could involve motions of confidence, such as the budget and estimates, and second order legislation which would involve free votes. It is argued that more independence for backbenchers to effectively amend and scrutinize legislation would force the government to offer more information and rely on persuasion rather than coercion. Concessions were to make parliament more responsive to popular needs. 3) Adoption of pre-legislative hearings as a routine procedure, involving parliament before a cabinet is committed would avoid embarrassing the government while bringing in more technical information and detail for the creation of policies. Committees and hearings have been brought in after first reading, though rarely. In 2002, after the Reform Party had come up with the idea of a 'democratic deficit,' Paul Martin used these terms to promote both these reforms and three more (Aucoin and Turnbull 2003). 4) Overhauling private member's bills to increase the capacity of individual MPs to initiate legislation. 5) Reforming the process of government appointments by letting parliament review them, making them more transparent. 6) Make the Ethics Officer more responsive to report to parliament. While others have suggested changing elections to proportional representation to force more coalitions.

According to Aucoin and Turnbull (2003) essential to the first five recommendations was the relaxation of party discipline. Freeing up debate with strong committees, possibly brought in after first reading, private member's bills, and the review of appointments would be unproductive if parliament continued to be partisan, and without getting rid of the confidence convention MPs would be forced to vote along party lines to maintain or obtain office. Even if party discipline was relaxed this may not do much, since out of loyalty and ambition or simply because of the fact that they got elected because of their parties' platform they would still toe the party line.

A History of the Ideologies of the Welfare State

It was only natural that the Reform Party would come up with the terms 'democratic deficit' since they were a populist party. Populism tends to believe the common folk know what's best for themselves and that elites are corrupt, unresponsive and have distorted views. The favorite reforms of populists are plebiscites or citizen's initiatives, referendums, and recalls. Participant democracy can be furthered through new communications devices such as websites and on-line consultations (Matsusaka 2005). Electronic referendums and plebiscites could bypass the legislature all together. The threat of a recall would supposedly force MPs to vote according to the preferences of their constituents, while more independence for MPs would allow them to do this. However, just because an MP is given their independence and a free vote does not mean they will vote the way their constituents want. This takes us into the distinction between the MP as a 'delegate' and as a 'trustee.'

298

A delegate is supposed to vote the way their constituents tell them to do.   A trustee is supposed to use their own judgement since they may be experts that know better about technical details. As Edmund Burke said 200 years ago "your representative owes you, not his industry only, but his judgement; and he betrays, instead of serving you, if he sacrifices it to your opinion." (as quoted in Stilborn 2002 p.16) Constituents should not triumph over the general good. The trustee seeks to define the national interest through deliberation and compromise. With reflective equilibrium there is feedback between general principles and details, such that an MP can rationally change their mind through discussion. Trustees would still have to show they are responsive to their constituents. The delegate position may have become more popular with the decline of deference to authority in Canada. But delegates would have to show how they can represent a heterogeneous riding, or interests that are not regionally

A History of the Ideologies of the Welfare State

bound such as religious, ethnic, or linguistic minorities. Both forms of independence would give more power to backbenchers, but can be seen as incompatible with the tradition of responsible government.

According to Brooks and Menard (2013 p.148) *"The constitutional principle that the prime minister and cabinet require the confidence of the elected House of Commons in order to govern* is called **responsible government**." The value behind this arrangement was to have strong executive authority with clear democratic accountability. It is Us versus Them between the Party of the government and the Parties of the opposition; when in the House each sits across a central aisle from the other. The Government had to be as strong enough to effectively act but still held responsible to answer to the elected representatives rather than just the king or queen. It kept a Manchester type parliament with the Governor General representing the crown, but was also the first step towards Canada's independence. Minority governments or a legislature with undisciplined parties and many independents would be unpredictable, the necessary compromises can blur the lines of accountability. The government is to have monopoly over legislation while the opposition has monopoly over criticism. "The opposition minority, uncompromised by participation in the government, is free to attack it." (Smith 1999 p.407) Only the executive can initiate and formulate policy. "The one-party majority is the condition of the potential of the system to produce strong and decisive administration." (Smith 1999 p.411) When there is a minority government there may be more space for amendments when the votes of backbenchers actually matter.

Johnathon Malloy (1996) argued there has been a conflict between expectations and the reality of the House of Commons. Those who expected the 1989 committee on the GST to be nonpartisan and have a real effect on formulating the legislation, such as the Chair Don Blenkarn, were disappointed by the constant petty partisan bickering. However, by having businesses articulate why they should not be subject to the GST, one came up with a good argument that got leaked to the media and indirectly affected the legislation, lowering the amount from 9% to 7%. Malloy suggested that a more realistic expectation about how the committee shaped public debate would have satisfied more of those involved. Policies and laws are primarily originated in the Prime Minister's Office with input from the civil service, listening primarily to opinion polls and special interests. MPs normally get a chance to only make minimal amendments and can't affect the government's priorities. Perhaps a shift in emphasis is needed. Maybe the role of the MP outside the House should be seen as more important: Caucasus, constituency offices, and the shaping of public opinion.

Canadian MPs serve four functions: law-making, scrutinizing the government, constituency work, and shaping public debate. Suggestions for making the legislature more relevant have included giving more power to backbenchers, the opposition and standing committees. These reforms would be useless if debate remained pre-set by partisanship. However, relaxing party discipline and compromising with the opposition would go against the intent of responsible government, which was to deliver an effective cabinet with clear lines of accountability. If we shifted our emphasis from legislation to outside the House, we could see MPs are quite capable of doing constituency work and helping articulate public debate. Therefore, MPs are not simply trained seals, at least not without qualification.

Bibliography

'The Role of a Member of Parliament'
www.parl.gc.ca/About/Parliament/GuideToHoC/role-e.htm

Aucion, Peter and Turnbull, Lori (2003) The democratic deficit: Paul Martin and parliamentary reform. Canadian Public Administration 46(4): 427-449.

Brooks, Stephan & Menard, Marc (2013) 'The Legislature' in Canadian Democracy: A Concise Introduction. Don Mills, Ontario: Oxford UP.

Franks, C. E. S. (1971) The Dilemma of Standing Committees of the Canadian House of Commons. Canadian Journal of Political Science IV(4): 461-476.

Lovink, J. A. A. (1973) Parliamentary reform and governmental effectiveness in Canada. Canadian Public Administration 16(1): 35-54.

Malloy, Johnathon (1996) Reconciling expectations and reality in House of Commons committees: The case of the 1989 GST inquiry. Canadian Public Administration 39(3): 314-335.

Matsusaka, John G. (2005) The eclipse of legislatures: Direct democracy in the 21st century. Public Choice 124(1 and 2): 157-177.

Smith, Jennifer (1999) Democracy and the Canadian House of Commons at the millennium. Canadian Public Administration 42(4): 398-421.

Stilborn, Jack (2002) The Roles of the Member of Parliament in Canada: Are They Changing? Ontario, Ottawa: Parliament Research Branch, Political and Social Affairs Division. www.parl.gc.ca/content/lop/researchpublications/prb0204-e.htm

Thomas, Paul G. (2010) 'Parliament and Legislatures: Central to Canadian Democracy?' in The Oxford Handbook of Canadian Politics ed. John C. Courtney and David E. Smith. New York, NY: Oxford UP.

Wolin, Sheldon (1960/2004) Politics and Vision. Woodstock, Oxfordshire: Princeton UP.